PINAY
Culture Bearers of the Filipino Diaspora

An anthology collected by the
Filipino Association of University Women
(FAUW)

Editors
Virgie Chattergy
Pepi Nieva

DEDICATION

To our mothers and grandmothers
Fathers and grandfathers
And our sons and daughters

ACKNOWLEDGEMENTS

The Filipino Association of University Women of Hawai'i
(FAUW) thanks

Virgie Chattergy, who birthed this collection with her
concept of cultural values and their transmission to the next
generations; and wrestled the stories into their fruition.

Rose Cruz Churma for project managing the collection
process.

Kit Zulueta for designing the book cover.

Pepi Nieva for final editing, layout, and publication.

The University of Hawai'i Hamilton Library for hosting our
initial talk story/sharing sessions, inspiring writers.

And all the writers who shared their talents and stories.
SALAMAT AND MAHALO.

CONTENTS
Foreword
Mothers, Fathers & Daughters

Spirit Worlds & Ancient Wisdoms

Finding Our Way

Next Generation

About FAUW
About the Cover Designer

FOREWORD

The impetus for this anthology, "PINAY: Culture Bearers of the Filipino Diaspora," began with a question:
What happens to traditional Philippine core values if Filipinos who live away from the country forget to remember them as they live out their lives? And if values were maintained, which ones would Filipinos NOT give up because in doing so, they would no longer be recognized as a Filipino, individually and/or collectively?

The Filipino Association of University Women (FAUW) sent out invitations to its members and their friends to meet and discuss these and similar questions.

There was considerable interest to review our core values. The major reference for the subject on Philippine core values came from Professor Virgilio Enriques' scholarly work on *Sikolohiyang Pilipino*. The first sessions focused on commonly known core values. However, due to the abstract nature of "values" as a concept, we shifted the focus on how these might be expressed in our lived experiences. Cultural values are expressed in behaviors, in our thoughts, in decisions we make or through our participation in customs and rituals. The anthology began to take shape. Potential writers emerged as we shared informally our remembrances of things Philippine or recalled how our Filipino orientation shaped our responses to people, things, and events.

Potential contributors were asked to write their personal stories about the extent to which they believed in, incorporated, and practiced Philippine values that they have learned themselves, directly or as taught by families and friends.

1

As a trigger to jog memories and provide a context for their narratives, we identified major life transitions that included a wide range of foci—from birth to death and everything in between. They could write about experiences related to any one or two of the following: Finding one's partner in life or issues of courtship/marriage; child-bearing and child rearing, becoming a parent, bringing up teenagers and their own memories of being one; caring for the elderly, handling crisis like the loss of a loved one, caring for the seriously ill, death, and end-of-life issues.

Using these possible references, they were to examine the beliefs, attitudes, practices, and rituals they drew on to deal with these situations. Where possible, they were to reflect on how a Filipino upbringing factors into how they approached these challenges/opportunities. Were these traditions and their underlying values of benefit? If so, in what way? Would they pass them on to the next generation? Modify or drop them altogether? Is being a Filipina an advantage or disadvantage when confronted with these transitions?

Three basic principles about writing provided additional incentive and encouragement: 1) everyone has a story to tell; 2) they were writing on a subject they knew about, intimately; and 3) they wrote with a purpose. Along with the first person, non-fiction narrative submissions, we accepted poems that addressed the overall theme.

The outcome is a variety of personal stories and poems that speak to the different aspects of a Filipino's belief system. The most popular theme running through these stories pertains to family relations—in good times, in challenging situations, in times of crisis and, through it all, the family stays together.

The narratives underscore the writers' pride in the importance of family, the Filipinos' resilience and independence when called for, strength of character and the ability to adapt while holding constant what they hold dear.

A question came up about why we focus on the women.

The answer comes from an anthropologist, Margaret Mead, who once wrote that cultures are slow to change but if there is change, watch the women. They are the culture bearers of a society. When they change, the likelihood of changes in societal attitudes and practices will be noticeable. Hence, we focused on women's thoughts, their practices and their fidelity (or not) to traditions.

It is one of FAUW's goals to promote an understanding of Filipino culture. This collection of lived experiences and personal accounts of our women will contribute, hopefully, to future generations' insights into the different aspects of a Pinay's life in diaspora.

Virgie Chattergy
Co-editor

This anthology is divided into four sections:

Mothers, Fathers & Daughters follows Filipinas as they reflect on family and its influence on their yesterdays, todays, and tomorrows.

The stories of *Spirit Worlds and Ancestral Wisdoms* indicate that the old ways can live on, even as they blend and evolve to fit our disparate environments.

Finding Our Way tells of resilience and transformation as Filipinas adapt and create their own circumstances in contemporary society. Most came to the United States and other parts of the world as young women beginning a new life in a new country.

Next Generation features the voices of a younger generation, those who grew up in Hawai'i immersed within two, sometimes clashing cultures, finding identity both Filipino and American.

Just like their experiences, the languages used in this book—English, Pilipino, other Philippine languages, and

3

Hawaiian—are interwoven and undifferentiated. We do not use italics to identify the "foreign" languages because they are not foreign to us, but innate, part and parcel of who we are, how we think, how we express ourselves.

PINAY also raises the question: Have we succeeded in transmitting our core values and principles? Is culture-bearing even important as we must assimilate to succeed? Is there a role for Filipino-ness within the dominant culture?

Perhaps our stories will bring some light to this discussion. Read and decide!

Pepi Nieva
Co-editor

MOTHERS, FATHERS
&
DAUGHTERS

Hawai'i plantation family.

One
AN EXTENSION OF SOLING
by Jenny Alconcel Quezon

There are a few constant reminders of Soling in my life: Her high pitched melodic laughter I sometimes would imitate to get a funny reaction from relatives; her love of bird of paradise plants and small coconut trees that lined our long driveway in our Kuliouou residence; the white and green houses that we grew up in; the way she cleared her nose due to allergies caused by dusting; her watermelon and egg fuyong that she learned to cook after attending Chinese cooking classes and tried first on her family when I was 11 years old.

We moved to Hawai'i in May, 1958 and it must have been a heart-wrenching, difficult decision to uproot all of us six children ranging in age from six to 20. To this day, I can still remember her crying out in pain at night whenever she had leg cramps from standing at the Philippine Handicrafts store to greet her customers at her first shop on Uluniu Street in Waikiki, and then, later, at her well-known store at the Ala Moana Shopping Center right next to Foodland. She owned this store for 17 years. She literally worked 16-hour days, first sorting merchandise that would arrive from the pier, and then managing the store from nine a.m. to nine p.m.

There were two older siblings in college, Solita and Romeo; Cecilio at St. Louis High School; and Angelina, Jenny, and Victoria at St. Augustine School, which was walking distance to her shop in Waikiki. I totally understand now why she had no time to attend school plays, volleyball games, piano recitals, honor roll presentations, or just to go window shopping. I remember during Halloween that she would bring home one box

6

Channeling Soling: Jenny and her mother.

each of our favorite candy, just so we would not nag her about allowing us to join our friends going from house to house in costumes. Each one of us had a favorite, and I would alternate between M&Ms and Milky Way.

After graduating from St. Augustine School, I was accepted to Maryknoll High School. I found out later that she allowed me to "choose" Sacred Hearts Academy because it was more convenient to ride the bus to 21st and Maunaloa Avenues, where we purchased our very first house after the shop opened at the Ala Moana Center. Later on, I found out that it was because Sacred Hearts was not a co-ed school.

I used to be extra sensitive when it seemed that I was the only one she would monitor about what time I got home from school or when she listened in on my phone calls. Sometimes I had to wear hand me downs from my oldest sister Solita to cut down on expenses. From accompanying my mother to the beauty shop every month, I learned how to set up hair with rollers, use sticky gel, cut bangs, and apply nail polish simply by observing how the beauticians did them. I was always willing to learn new things like ironing my Dad's dress pants with just ONE straight line in the front. Dad praised me because although I was second to the youngest, I took it upon myself to choose that chore.

Eventually, as we got older, we had to go to the Ala Moana store after school to help straighten out the merchandise on display. For some reason, I got stuck with dusting and organizing the wood carvings although Soling had three full-time salesclerks by this time. I truly believe that this was her way of keeping an eye on us girls. On weekends, we would clean the house. I never learned how to cook since Soling would rush to cook for eight people three meals a day on weekends. It was never my favorite chore to learn. I distinctly remember that when we first moved to Hawai'i, I decided to wash the dishes and learned for the first time to throw in the wash. The dishes were no problem but I had no idea about measuring the soap for the clothes. My Dad once again conveniently mentioned to the other five children over breakfast the following morning to pitch in more. "Look at my Enny, only 11 and she is aware of how much help your mother needs around the house."

My nickname, when Dad was in a very good mood, was Enny but when he wanted to emphasize that he was not too happy with something or other, the LOUDER the J would be in my name. When there was a school dance or a birthday party to attend, we all knew that it was a good sign when he whistled as he was getting ready for work. It meant he would say yes.

For me, at that time, Soling's way of showing affection was giving us six kids our weekly allowance of $20 each, and buying new clothes on sale at Sears or Liberty House. It took a long time to dawn on me that she really and truly worked her butt off to support all six of us in the style to which we were accustomed back in Gilmore, Quezon City with the household help. She must have felt guilty for uprooting all of us. After representing the Philippines in the New York and Seattle World's Fair four years in a row, she made the decision not to ship the leftover goods back to the Philippines. Instead she had them shipped straight to Hawai'i to open a store.

Four of us sisters attended St. Paul's College in Manila first, then transferred to the school campus in Quezon City since it was more logical after we moved to 7th Street only seven blocks away. The nuns provided spiritual direction, and I received first honor/place in Religion. I would go to Catholic church with my Dad for the seven or eight o'clock morning mass and then go with Soling to her Methodist church. I did not know that a Catholic was not supposed to attend a Protestant service, that it was considered a venial sin. I just felt compelled to keep Soling company, and I enjoyed their singing the prayers. My two older brothers chose to become Protestants later in life.

Soling paid for a piano teacher, Miss Lara, who came to the house on Saturdays for six piano lessons. For some reason, two siblings would find excuses not to be available for lessons. Miss Lara was very encouraging, and so rather than wasting

9

Soling's hard-earned money, I took three lessons on Saturdays and continued piano lessons until we moved to Hawai'i. Soling would play a piano selection entitled "Love and Devotion" on early Saturday mornings and I told Miss Lara to teach me to play it.

When we first arrived in Honolulu, Soling paid for our Philippine folk dance lessons with Miss Aurelia Viernes. My piano lessons came later with Mr. James Feurring. However, I did not continue my voice lessons to save on additional expenses. We were featured on "Fiesta Filipina" and I was invited to play the piano on Mr. Cacatian's radio show. To this day, I think that this was the start of my love of our Filipino culture, learning about different regional dances and the costumes to wear with the dances. I also loved seeing Soling's beautiful, expensive Tesoro's and other designer embroidered gowns whenever she would return from her buying trips. This is probably why I also have new outfits made whenever my best friend Ruth Llacuna goes on her annual two-month long vacations to Paoay, Ilocos Norte. Sewing one skirt and two tops with panuelo are incredibly inexpensive there. The cost of the fabric used is three times more than the cost for sewing them.

I was overweight in my younger days because Soling would set the dessert trays next to our main dishes. We all developed a sweet tooth, and this is the price we are paying: Type 2 diabetes. But it is also a genetic thing, along with high blood pressure, high cholesterol, heart disease, and cancer, which run in both sides of the family. Two years ago, I made a decision to attend the nutrition class at Straub; it took me that long to re-learn about proper diet and weight. As a result, I am now 30 pounds lighter and I look much better in pictures whenever I am asked to sing "Hawai'i Pono'i" at functions. The best part is that I can wear size medium now instead of XL on top. My older siblings used to tease me about being overweight, and Dad even affectionately nicknamed me "Piggly Wiggly" until middle school.

My Mom passed away at 59. Despite her degree in

Pharmacy, she never took the time to go for annual check ups, pap smears, or mammograms. She said she had no time because she was raising six children. When she got sick, I had to track down my oldest brother, Romeo, through the American Red Cross. He was traveling as an agent, promoting and representing Outrigger Hotel and Tours. Since two older siblings had moved to the mainland, Dad and I took turns to be with Mom at the cancer unit during her last few months. One day, Dad asked me to go home to make some coffee for visitors. When I opened the front door, a strange sound came from our refrigerator. The phone rang. The nurse said that Dad told her to tell me, "No need for the coffee, just come back to Straub."

Returning to my Mom's ER room was the most devastating experience in my life. The nurse didn't tell me what to expect, and I saw a bloated something underneath bed sheets. I remember asking the nurse where my Mom was. When she pointed to the sheet, I realized my Mom was gone. I literally got weak in the knees and fainted. I could not believe that at 59 years old, in spite of two major surgeries to "save" her and two chemo sessions for her fourth-stage lymphoma cancer, she DIED. I could not say this word for a long time, especially when I had to be the one to tell my oldest sister Solita to fly to Hawai'i.

I could not sleep without the light on, and on the ninth day right after the funeral, I woke up in a cold sweat. I described to my husband Paul and my siblings the dream I had of Mom, hugging me from head to foot and how she pinched my eyes shut when I felt like I wanted to see her image. I just knew this was her way of saying goodbye, since she never showed any physical affection when we were growing up.

I could not breast feed my one-year-old son Justin while Mom was in the hospital from February, 1976 to the day she passed away on September 19, 1976. Dr. Mario Bautista, one of Mom's closest friends on the Philippine Cultural Foundation Board of Directors explained that the emotions I was going

11

through at that time made it impossible to breast feed. Thank God for Enfamil formula and disposable diapers, so unlike the time our oldest Chris was born (1968) when I had to wash cloth diapers everyday.

In so many ways, I now know that I am the extension of Soling. Whenever I put up my hair up in a French twist after Mom died, Dad would ask that I not do that. Of all his daughters, I look a lot like Mom. As I look through some old photos of Mom in college, my three sons and two grand children agree that there is a strong resemblance. Not only with her smiley eyes, but also in her taste for embroidered clothes, her love of formal events and in meeting VIP's and celebrities, her love of music and folk dances. My memory of her is probably the reason I have stayed involved in various Filipino organizations as a volunteer since 1984, when my youngest son Travis turned five and started attending preschool.

To this day, I sometimes think and reflect about why she did not want me to marry my husband: Too young according to her standards. He is Visayan. He came back wounded from Vietnam. She always felt that I should have been the one to marry a doctor or a lawyer. You see, one sister married Senator Ruperto Kangleon's son from Leyte, a former Quezon City neighbor, and my older sister Lina married the son of a Philippine Military Academy officer from Baguio. Mom would make a joke of it when introducing my husband Paul and say, "This one (as she pointed me out) married a son of sakada."

At the end, however, since Paul and I visited Straub every day, she finally made peace with my husband and told him "you are my favorite son-in-law," and asked him to ignore the way she treated him. She realized that Paul could do things around her Kuliouou house, such as replacing the tiles on the long hallway, buying toilet seat covers, and assisting in building the front fence. Paul also volunteered to pick her up from Ala Moana at 9:45 p.m. instead of her having to catch a cab when she needed a ride home at night. Paul started work at seven in the morning, so she appreciated his offer.

After raising our three sons and now my two adorable grand children, Kai and Rhea, I realize that Mom wanted the best for me, without having to struggle through the early years of marriage with Paul's Vietnam-related injuries and having to work two jobs for 28 years. Paul and I made a pact that our three sons would attend private school and made sure they all finished college. Thank God that we have been blessed with their partial academic scholarships since high school. Chris graduated from St. Louis High School and Loyola Marymount University in Los Angeles. Justin and Travis both graduated from Punahou School and University of Hawai'i. All three sons realize that we worked long hours to pay for their tuition since kindergarten. Justin and Travis decided to stay in Hawai'i for college. That way, Paul and I could each work just one job and still support the family comfortably.

Paul retired from Hickam Air Force Base, Civil Engineering Division, in 2004 after 18 years. He retired early due to needed emergency surgeries resulting from his Vietnam-related injuries. I retired from State government after 30 years, and have been working at the Hawai'i legislative sessions for the last eight years.

I wrote this in loving memory of Soledad Arre Alconcel (December 22, 1917 to September 19, 1976), who obtained a college degree (majored in Pharmacy) from the Philippine Women's Normal College in Manila and owned Philippine Handicrafts, Inc. from 1958 to 1976. In her will, she requested that her family run the business at the Ala Moana Shopping Center five more years after her death. The store closed in 1982. In Ermita, Manila, my mom was the proprietor of Solita's Embroidered Baby Dresses (which was expanded to include embroidered table cloths, runners, barongs, kimonas and dresses) until 1958 when she moved to Hawai'i.

In addition, this is a tribute to my father, Philippine Ambassador Trinidad Quitevis Alconcel (November 30, 1915 to June 17, 2004). He was a corporate lawyer at Castillo, Alconcel and Manalo in Manila before joining the Department of Foreign Affairs. He holds the longest tenure as consul general at the Philippine Consulate in Hawai'i (1966-1972, and 1976-1984). He later became ambassador to Argentina for seven years, and retired from the foreign service after 42 years. My father graduated from high school at the age of 12, and successfully completed three college degrees and passed the bar exam before the World War II broke out in the Philippines. He was a sugar technologist and chemist before working as a lawyer in Manila.

My husband and I are enjoying retirement, continuing to pray hard for good health and success for everyone in their family. We remain volunteers for community projects at the Philippine Consulate, Filipino Community Center, the Aloha United Way, and Hawai'i Food Bank.

Jenny Alconcel Quezon, born in Manila and raised in Gilmore, Quezon City, moved to Hawai'i in 1958 when her mother, Soledad Arre Alconcel uprooted the entire family instead of returning her goods back from the New York World's Fair where she represented the Philippines from 1954 to 1958. Jenny attended St. Paul College of Manila and Quezon City and transferred to St. Augustine's School then Sacred Hearts Academy in Honolulu. In 1974, she earned her BBA double majoring in PIR and Management from the University of Hawai'i at Manoa. Happily married to her high school sweetheart, Paul Quezon, a decorated combat-wounded Vietnam veteran, since December 3, 1966, she's been blessed with three sons (Christopher, Justin, and Travis) and two grand children, Kaikane and Rhea.

Two
SEARCHING FOR MY MOTHER'S PAST
By Dr. Belinda A Aquino

The title of this piece, especially written for Mother's Day, is a bit melodramatic, if not enigmatic. But it captures the essence of my thoughts about my mother. I consider her passing away in 1967 as my first major crisis and it has haunted me ever since. Her death left a great void which I've been seeking, probably unconsciously, to fill all these years in an effort to redefine the meaning of my own life.

Perhaps it is her example that led me to advocacy for human and civil rights while ensuring that Philippine culture and history is passed on and studied seriously via the institution I spearheaded for decades, the Philippine Studies Department at the University of Hawai'i Manoa.

Her Young Life

Her name was Teresa Ducusin Ancheta before she married my father, Modesto Laudencia Aquino, from the town of San Fernando in the province of La Union in Northern Luzon. Both were products of the turn of the 20th century, emerging from the old world of Spanish dogmatism and repression into the relatively more open and freer, but equally confining in its own way, American "manifest destiny." Both were caught in the turmoil of cultural transition, filled with uncertainty and violence as the Philippine-American War raged during their childhood, bringing much death and destruction, not only to their town but also to the whole country. And this is where my mother's story begins. It was not exactly a happy one.

What comes out from all this searching about my

15

mother's past is a portrait of a child caught in the political upheaval, punctuated by extreme adversity in a time of cholera, dysentery, smallpox, influenza, and other diseases that decimated her family, including her parents and many of her close relatives. Death was all around her as a child and in the end, only she and a younger brother, Pablo, survived. That survival was probably an act of God, but it was also a tribute to faith, fortitude, determination, and good old Ilokano resilience. With both their parents gone, my mother took on the responsibility of taking care of her brother until he was old enough to leave for the U.S. for school.

My mother was my first teacher, teaching me the alphabet by pointing at the headlines of the Manila Times. She would put me on her knee and point at a letter and say, "This is A" or m, or whatever letter she was pointing at. Or she would put me to sleep by singing mostly American folk songs by Stephen Foster and other composers such as "Old Folks at Home," "Home on the Range," "La Golondrina," and so on. She went to school with the Thomasites as her teachers.

Now that I look back at my own childhood, I often wonder how she managed to acquire a basic education and to qualify as one of several nursing student pioneers from the Ilocos region recruited by the colonial administration of the Philippine General Hospital (PGH). How she got from San Fernando to Manila, which is about 160 miles away, and how she adjusted to life in the big city, I'll never know.

By the time I was old enough to understand, I was going to Manila myself and never got to know the full details of my mother's early life. In those days, parents and children never really talked at length with one another, unlike today. It was only during snatches of vacation time when I would go back to the province that I began to piece together bits and pieces of her life, as told sporadically by her, my father, and other older relatives. Still, I felt I never got a complete picture, mainly because I was always away, either inside or outside the country.

A Pioneer Nursing Student

When she entered PGH as one of the new recruits from all over the country, she stayed in one of the original buildings of the University of the Philippines. One of her teachers was what would be called a racist today. When the teacher was displeased with the performance of my mother and her classmates, she would utter such vulgar statements like, "You're good for nothing" or "why don't you just go back to your province and plant camotes?" Because of the hardships they underwent, six of the student nurses tried to commit suicide; only one succeeded in taking her own life.

The students endured the humiliation and insults—but not for long. Resentment grew in the student ranks and in time they decided to stop working and walk out to protest the overly strict disciplinary control and punishment meted to erring students.

On September 13, 1916, when my mother and her classmates were already seniors (nursing took only three years then to complete), the nurses went on a strike—all 120 of them with just a few staying behind. Years later, my mother gave different, but not conflicting, versions of the strike, e.g. "We went on strike" to "There was a strike" to "We were sent home." I was surprised to learn that as early as then, Filipino students already had an activist inclination and were ready to stand up against injustice. The strike was fateful in my own personal life, as I will explain below.

Marriage Intervenes

The strike went on for a long time, not just days but months. My mother went back to San Fernando to wait for her orders to report back to work. Meanwhile, my father-to-be, who was a senior law student at the Liceo de Manila, also left Manila for the province at the time my mother was there. As fate would have it, my father, a persistent young chap, proposed to marry my mother. This put a hold on my mother's plans because the school of nursing then had a policy not to admit

17

married students. So, what to do?

She stayed in the province and started raising a family. My father left school as well and never took the bar exam. The joke in the family was that he left Manila because he was fleeing from another girlfriend there. As far as I could remember, however, this was never a subject of much conversation in the family. I think my mother was disappointed, probably embarrassed, that she did not finish her degree because she got married instead. And my father, who I gathered had a lot of girlfriends, was not bragging about his exploits either.

The Menopausal Baby

When my parents had their seventh child, my mother said that was more than enough. But her story wasn't over. It seemed that my father wanted one more baby who he could name his "junior." In retrospect, that seemed very strange because he could have named one their three sons after him. Instead he named them Agustin, Pericles, and Napoleon. To cut a long story short, the now aging Mrs. Aquino gave birth to one more baby, but it was a girl! Not a potential Junior. She worried a lot because she was already 46 and was told that menopausal babies might have some behavioral problems after they were born. The spaces between the older siblings were one-and-a-half to two years, and this one came after seven years. It was unusual to have another baby when you're already 46. But my father was desperate, it would seem.

I was that menopausal baby! It turned out that I became his favorite child. He started to call me "Billy" for some reason. Perhaps he still couldn't forget that deep in his heart, he would have preferred a boy. One time one of my friends stopped by our house to look for Lindy and my father said that there was no one by that name!

Her Legacy

My mind keeps going back to that Great Nurses' Strike as I began to recall it in my imagination. Perhaps if it didn't happen, I would never have been born. My mother would have gone on and graduated and probably married a doctor instead of a lawyer-to-be. Maybe she may never have returned to our hometown with an unfinished career, but finished and went on to the U.S. Is there such a thing as fate or destiny after all?

During the University of the Philippines Centennial in 2008, I donated a Professorial Chair to the UP College of Nursing in honor of my mother. She sacrificed a lot—her life, her career, and her happiness just to take care of all of us. And she never complained. The least I could do was to memorialize her legacy. She and the other hardy pioneers of her generation were trailblazers in building nursing as a modern profession at a crucial time in our nation's confrontation with modernization, especially of science and health issues.

By pulling that strike, they were making history without knowing it. My mother's generation was part of the core group from whom that great institution we now know as the Philippine General Hospital emerged. I salute their courage and, though the strike cut short my mother's nursing career, it was a correct and great decision that eventually led to reforms and the Filipinization of nursing as a modern professional field. My mother and her fellow pioneer student nurses contributed immensely to that monumental effort.

Still, there's so much I don't know about my mother's meaningful and productive life…and my search for her past will continue.

 *An internationally recognized authority on contemporary Philippine affairs, Lindy Aquino received her Ph.D. in Political Science from Cornell University as a Ford Foundation fellow, M.A. in Political Science and Public Administration from the University of Hawai'i as an East-West Center scholar, and B.A. in English from the University of the Philippines. She is the past Director of the Center for Philippine Studies at the University of Hawai'i at Manoa (1975-2009) and Vice President for Public Affairs at the University of the Philippines (1989-91).*

Three
PASSING ON THE ADVICE AND EXAMPLE
OF MY PARENTS
by Angie Dytioco Santiago

Growing up, we all remember some of the valuable advice our parents gave us. My parents emphasized the writings of the famed Philippine national hero Dr. Jose Rizal. Dr. Rizal wrote, "Ang hindi lumingon sa pinanggalingan ay hindi makakarating sa paroroonan," which means, "Those who do not learn from the past, or who are not thankful of those who helped in the past, will not succeed."

This advice had a profound meaning to my parents, Angel and Rubing Dytioco. By their love, perseverance, and hard work they demonstrated to the family the values they wanted their children to practice.

Angel and Rubing had been sweethearts since they were teenagers. Angel was a gas attendant and Rubing was a domestic helper working for her aunt. After graduating from Hagonoy Institute in Bulacan, Dad moved to live with his uncle Geraldo Socco in Pasay City and worked as a messenger. In 1955, Dad took the U.S. Navy's entrance test and passed. Passing the test was one of Dad's happiest moments, but his Navy career was put on hold for a year due to a medical issue. Finally, on February 14, 1956, at the age of 23, Angel was accepted into the U.S. Navy as a mess attendant. Although Dad had mixed emotions about leaving home, he knew that this was an opportunity he could not pass up, if he was to have a better and brighter future.

Angel Dytioco spent five years as a Navy steward before going home to marry his childhood sweetheart.

Arriving in San Diego, California, Dad spent three months in basic training and school. He was amazed at how modern San Diego was compared to his hometown. Dad's first duty station was in New Orleans, Louisiana, where he witnessed first-hand racism and racial segregation. When riding the bus, to avoid getting into trouble, Dad would sit in the back row with the non-whites and avoided making eye contact with anyone.

After a year in New Orleans, Dad was stationed in Pearl Harbor, Hawai'i. When Dad first arrived in Honolulu, he knew this was where he wanted to raise a family someday. After serving five years as a Navy steward, Dad was getting homesick and opted to leave the service. He received an honorable discharge and returned home to Hagonoy to marry Rubing, the love-of-his-life.

Blessed with four children—Noel, Leo, Solly, and Angie—Mom and Dad sought to improve our family's situation. Dad sacrificed, and leaving his family in the Philippines for a while, used his G.I. Bill benefits to pursue a University of Hawai'i Bachelor's degree in Agriculture. He was a full-time student, living on a $250 a month veteran's stipend, most of which he sent home to his family and to his parents and two sisters. With little money for his own expenses, Dad was blessed to have two wonderful friends in Buddy Gendrano and Melga Torre who cared for him and brought him food whenever he was sick.

During college, Dad joined the Peace Corps and became a Tagalog language instructor on the Big Island and Moloka'i under Dr. Teresita Ramos and Vicky Bunye. In May 1971, Dad became the first of his siblings to graduate from college.

In November 1972, Dad successfully petitioned for Mom and the children to come to Hawai'i. Dad went on to work for the City & County of Honolulu as a plant propagator and later retired from the federal government as a tractor operator after 30 years of service. Mom retired as a professional seamstress and the family's finance "guru" in addition to being a fulltime babysitter for her two grandsons, Aven and Damien. Dad

22

always enjoyed the outdoor life, so in January 2001, he returned to work for the City's Department of Parks and Recreation where, at the age of 82, he still enjoyed going to work every day.

We lived a simple and humble life growing up, but felt blessed and not at all disadvantaged. We did everything as a family, from growing vegetables to fishing, crabbing, picking mangoes, avocados, sampalok, or kamatsile. We helped our Dad with his yard maintenance business, and did janitorial work at various financial institutions.

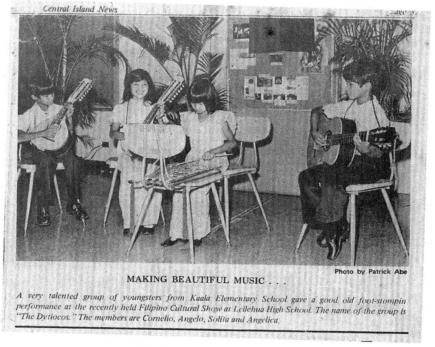

Central Island News

MAKING BEAUTIFUL MUSIC . . .

Photo by Patrick Abe

A very talented group of youngsters from Kaala Elementary School gave a good old foot-stompin performance at the recently held Filipino Cultural Show at Leilehua High School. The name of the group is "The Dytiocos." The members are Cornelio, Angelo, Solita and Angelica.

The Dytioco family rondalla.

Dad and Mom also took us on family trips to our native land to visit relatives and reconnect with our Filipino cultural heritage and roots. Whenever we vacationed in the Philippines, my two kuya, ate, and I would take up music lessons from Lobing Dionisio, who taught us how to play the guitar, banduria, laud, bamboo flute, marimba, and xylophone.

In this way the Dytioco Rondalla (musical ensemble) was formed, with Dad as manager and Mom as our wardrobe designer. From the early 1970s to the late 1980s, we performed at political fundraiser events, at pageants, for school May Day Programs, at shopping malls, cultural parades, and for the "Filipino Fiesta" television show with Tata Respicio. We even got to perform at the Waikiki Shell! Through our rondalla, our parents showed us how to give back to the community.

Mom and Dad taught us humility and not to forget where we came from, to accept every learning opportunity, to be thankful to people who help us along the way, and to always give back or pay forward.

Our parents always told us that "charity begins at home." But their charity went far beyond our home. It meant helping out loved ones back in the Philippines by sending monies so that relatives could attend schools or start their own businesses. They often have gone out of their way to help someone in need. When people are struggling or sick, Mom and Dad do what they can to help out. They have exemplified the virtues of being kind to others, giving back to the community, treating people with respect, and overcoming obstacles. Mom and Dad have engrained in us good work ethics, strong family values, and a resounding pride in our Philippine culture and heritage.

The words of Dr. Rizal and the advice of my parents to learn from the past, help others, and be thankful of those who help us—these set of values is the legacy I hope to pass on to my children and their children.

Angie Dytioco Santiago is an Equal Opportunity Specialist for the City & County of Honolulu. She and her husband Steven have two sons, Aven and Damien. Angie enjoys traveling, photography, excercising, cooking, hiking, and volunteering at community events. She currently serves as an officer for various Filipino organizations in Hawai'i.

Four
FOUR TO SIX HOURS
By Michelle Cruz Skinner

The day my mother had heart surgery, I drove her to Kuakini Hospital. It was cool at 5:30 in the morning, and I'd taken the day off from work. We were both nervous although I tried not to show it. The streets were quiet, the ride the same. At the hospital, we reviewed the final pre-operation forms, my mother was prepped, and the surgeon, already wearing his scrubs, re-introduced himself.

The idea that my mother needed an operation still did not seem real. She was the one who took up jogging, ("running" as it was called then) when I was in elementary school. She sprouted her own alfalfa that she put in our marinated cucumber and tomato salads. She would loudly proclaim, "I'm so tired of meat!"—really just in reference to the preponderance of meat and potatoes in my dad's Midwestern diet—and cook up pinakbet with just a touch of pork, or my childhood favorite, sinigang with hipon. When she hit her sixties, she gave up jogging for long, rapid walks through Manoa. When I stopped by her house, she'd give me homemade energy bars to take home. When my children visited, she had snacks of sliced fruit ready in the refrigerator.

But my mother had a defective heart valve and two partially blocked arteries. The valve would need to be replaced. "What kind of valve should I get?" she asked and went over her options with me. "You should get the one that will last the longest." My husband added, "You're going to live forever."

My mother prepared for surgery in the orderly way she had all her life: She got blessed by a priest; made sure both her

25

bank and retirement plan knew her beneficiaries; and got her cousin to fly in from Canada to stay with her after I had to return to work.

So, everything was ready. "We estimate four to six hours," the doctor said, echoing what we'd already been told by the nurse prepping my mother that morning. So my mother went into the operating room, and I went to the cafeteria for four to six hours. I ate my rice, eggs, and sausage and watched two nurses saunter in for coffee. They picked up the muffins, turning them to inspect for blueberries, then picked up some granola bars. They eventually settled for yogurt. I envied their completely normal day. I tried reading a book while drinking my weak coffee, but kept reading the same two pages over and over. More hospital staff arrived, talking about meetings, traffic, colleagues, chit-chatting with the cashier. I read the two pages over yet again. Waiting for someone to get out of surgery, there is always the possibility of death. It's built into the process. The patient is put under and should, under normal circumstances, arise. But then, there's always that other possibility. I couldn't sit still any longer. It had only been 40 minutes.

I stood outside watching morning traffic on Kuakini Street, in front of the hospital. Cars, trucks, and a bus surged past in both directions, clogging the two-lane street. What was there to do? I decided to walk. But, keeping in mind my terrible sense of direction, I started heading back towards my mother's apartment, a route I knew well. Instead of seeing everything through a car window, I was seeing it up close. There were actually houses tucked away from the street, a gate that leads further into a park, and a bridge below that was a stream.

At the corner of Nuuanu and Kuakini, I turned left, still retracing the route to my mother's apartment. Near the Chevron station, I should have headed right, but the walk up Nuuanu was a straight shot, no possibility of getting lost, even for me. A breeze blew down the mountain, ruffling the distant tree branches, a canopy of green along the roadside waving invitingly at me. I shivered in the seven a.m. breeze and pulled my jacket closed, then began walking uphill. And that's how I found Oahu Cemetery.

Going to cemeteries has always seemed to me a very Filipino thing. My husband has been to a cemetery at least three times to visit my dead relatives. That's more times than he's been to a cemetery for his relatives as the only time I've ever known him to go for them was on the occasion of his uncle's funeral. Perhaps it's a Catholic thing. All visits to the Philippines have included at least one visit to the cemetery. When our children balked at this expectation, my husband simply explained, "You have to visit all your relatives, living and dead."

"I used to visit the cemetery three or four times a year," I told our kids.

"Why?"

"To pay them respects."

Or as my oldest aunt explained: "They gave us everything, so we need to thank them." By this, she was referring to the rice fields we still own in my Lolo's (grandfather) hometown, the house in Makati, and the money in the various banks. But, she could also have been referring to the history that had led up to us.

I've always been bad at remembering details of family history. Who is related to whom and how does that connect them to us? But that is, perhaps, the only thing I like about cemeteries—the history.

There is something intriguing about cemeteries: The dates carved in old stones showing the span of a life; the carved images; an angel; a rose; palms in prayer; the occasional rough stone portrait; and the grandeur of mausoleums that tell the viewer what mattered to the family and to the era. Walking alone around Oahu cemetery, I read the names softly to myself, letting them roll around on my tongue. Old names, familiar names: Lorrin, Martha, Damon, Hiram, Mary, Kealoha, and on and on—names that made me wonder about the lives attached to them. What did they love? Did she have long brown hair and play the piano? Did she wake up early some mornings to cook fried rice for her children and her grand children? Did the boy have siblings who lived much longer and settled far from here?

After an hour of stumbling amongst all the people and their lives, I walked back to Kuakini and wrote. I wrote down the things my mother had told me about her life and the things she had done. She used to give me ginger tea with sugar when I was younger and had to stay home when sick. When she planned to go to the beach, it was for the whole day. So, she had a list of "beach things" taped to one of the cabinets in our kitchen. She hated to sew but loved to cook. She taught me her recipe for adobo, the most important part of which is, according to her, using more vinegar than shoyu. She loved to put chili pepper in all her food. She had left the Philippines to study in the U.S. on scholarship. Her roommate in college had been an international student from Indonesia. They made friends with another student from Korea and learned to love kimchee. Years later, she continued to exchange Christmas cards with them. She had learned to drive in Ithaca, New York.

She had left the Philippines to study in the U.S. on scholarship. Her roommate in college had been an international student from Indonesia. They made friends with another student from Korea and learned to love kimchee. Years later, she continued to exchange Christmas cards with them. She had learned to drive in Ithaca, New York.

Nothing was organized. It was all in bits and pieces that suddenly needed to be set on paper.

My mother did recover and even went back to work. I did end up writing parts of her story, her family's story in essays. I have written about going with my grandfather back to his hometown of Teresa, near Manila. I have written about my mother saving junk mail letters, so she could use the blank backs as scratch paper. I've created fictional versions of my mother who feed their families, lose their tempers, and buy large quantities of sale items from Long's.

Michelle with daughters Anna and Maya and Lola Eppie Skinner.

There is a lot of her story that I don't know. And it is out of reach. About three years after the surgery, my mother was diagnosed with dementia. The disease progressed quickly. Within two years she couldn't remember basic facts or cook all the foods she used to cook. Helping me in the kitchen, she often lost track of what she was doing such as slicing cucumbers, or setting out dishes. Two years later she could not remember my name. Then she was bedridden until she quietly passed away.

But before that, I did sit down one summer and tried to tell her story. I looked at her old Philippine passports, birth certificates, photo albums, and yearbooks. The story could not only be about the woman with dementia but the woman she had been.

In the midst of this, my younger daughter needed to write a family story for a high school English class. The class was reading *The Joy Luck Club*. For a final assignment, she had to interview a family member. She'd chosen to write about her Lola, her Filipino grandmother, who by this point could no longer talk. So, my daughter talked to me instead. Could I tell her about some specific part of Lola's life?

Sitting on her bed, we talked about Lola. Her father used

to take her for walks along Manila Bay so the sea air could help her asthma. In first grade, she used to sneak away from school and go back to the neighborhood and play with her friends. Then her mother caught her. When World War II began, her family was still living in Manila. Her pet dog, Laban, was run over by a Japanese army jeep. Her uncle held a funeral for the dog. During the war, her family left for Teresa, my grandfather's hometown. There, they wrapped up their silverware and few valuables and buried them, to be retrieved after the war. For most of the war, they lived on arroz caldo, a chicken and rice soup that was mostly watery rice. For years after the war, she refused to eat arroz caldo.

My daughter retold the stories well: The dusty street on which her Lola's dog died; and the clink of the silverware as it was dropped into the hole in the ground. I wonder about the stories that someday she and her sister would tell others. The stories will be different. They will remember their Lola differently. By then, there will also be stories about myself and their father, the bits and pieces that will be remembered.

Two hours I spent writing, off and on, about my mother while she was in surgery. And I've spent many more hours writing her into stories and essays. As part of the span of her life, it's not a lot. But, maybe it's enough. The stories of Marciano, Potenciana, Maria, Epifania, the Capili family, the towns of Pateros and Teresa, will always be there in our stories of ourselves, an undercurrent even when they cease to be named.

Michelle Cruz Skinner was born in Manila, Philippines. She has published two collections of short stories—Balikbayan: A Filipino Homecoming *and* In The Company Of Strangers—*as well as a novel,* Mango Seasons. *Her work has appeared in* Manoa *and* Bamboo Ridge *magazines.*
She currently teaches at Punahou School.

Five

MY WALK DOWN THE AISLE

by Linda Bahinting Abuel

When I was a young girl, I loved to watch wedding scenes in Philippine movies and dream of my very own wedding someday. I imagined myself dressed like a princess in a white lace wedding gown with its long sweep train, a long lace veil with dainty white flowers draped over my hair, my face somewhat covered by a soft white mesh. I wore a pair of white satin gloves, my Mom's charming necklace, and a pair of white high-heeled shoes. I held a sweet-scented bouquet of white roses and orchids and I fancied riding on the white limousine that would take me to the church. I pictured the church filled with family and friends, I could hear the church choir singing my wedding song and, of course, myself at the end of the wedding procession. I was excited at the thought of walking down the aisle fully adorned with white flowers, with my father who would hand me over to my future husband. My dream ended at that point as I could not picture who my groom would be.

I am the eldest in a brood of four girls and two boys. Our parents did not have much to offer in terms of material things, but they had all the love and the dream of a happy and comfortable life for their children. Dad worked tirelessly to send us to private schools and we all graduated from college. Mom did the best she could to provide us with a happy home. They both regarded education as the only legacy they could give to us and so school work was our priority over everything else.

I have no stories to tell my grand children of teenage

parties, cutting classes and wild escapades which most teenagers venture into these days. You may say my teen life was boring. However, at school, I was an active member of dance, drama and glee clubs, entered declamation and oratorical contests, and wrote for my school paper. I excelled in what I did, was in the honors' society, and earned a number of medals and awards. My Dad was very proud of me. My Dad was the traditional Filipino father who strictly "guarded" me from boys who came my way. I got the brunt of it as I am the oldest among his daughters. And so in my young mind, I had always thought that I may never get married if my father had his way. Truth be told, I never dated until I was past 20 years old and was already gainfully employed. And those "dates" I had were secrets I kept from my Dad.

I remember my college senior prom at the University of Santo Tomas in Manila, Philippines. I was scared to ask for my father's permission to go, so I toyed with the idea of not attending. Besides I was uncomfortable in asking someone to escort me. But I did not want to miss this one occasion. Everyone in my class was preparing for it. My Mom coached me on how to talk to my Dad, and thanks to divine intervention, I was given permission to go as long as I promised to be home by 10 o'clock. My father also agreed that I invite my next-door neighbor to be my escort. It was my first time to ask a guy a favor and I remember rehearsing what to say and how to react if he declined. My "script" was effective, my neighbor said "yes," and so off we went to the prom.

I do not remember now if I danced and had fun, but I remember looking at my watch every now and then to check the time. The party ended a little past nine o'clock and as one of the Council officers who was in-charge of the party, I had to stay behind to help tidy up the place. At that time, proms were held at the UST gymnasium. I could not calm myself down as my curfew drew near for I knew I could not be home by 10 o'clock that night. On the way home I was praying again for divine intervention that my Dad would be sleeping when I got

32

home. But no, not even Lady Luck favored me with my request. When I got home close to midnight, I saw the lights were still up at our house and as I was tiptoeing my way up the stairs, the door opened and my father was right in my face. The next thing I remembered was falling down a few flights of stairs in my prom gown and I was hurting from a slap in my face. Needless to say, I cried and pleaded with my Dad and explained why I broke my promise. To this day, I do not know if what I said made sense to him, because we never spoke about the incident after that night.

I will never forget that night; it was a vivid memory of my Dad's control over me. I must say that I was not rebellious nor hated my Dad for what happened because I truly understood where he was coming from. But my fear of my Dad was intensified by that incident and it caused me to distance myself from and not be open with him.

I met my husband Conrad at the CPA firm where we both worked. I was an apprentice in the audit department and he worked in the administrative office. We dated for less than two years before he left for the United States in the fall of 1975. My Dad knew of Conrad as just my friend, because I did not have the courage to tell him about my romantic relationship. I made excuses not to invite Conrad over at our house because felt he was uncomfortable being with my family. I could see that in the few times he came to visit me. In short, my relationship with him was a secret from my parents even when he left for the US. We had a long distance relationship which I favored because I did not have to look over my shoulders anymore. But I had to get to the mailbox before anyone else did to make sure his letters did not get into the "wrong" hands.

My apprenticeship at the audit firm did not require me to sit for a CPA license, but it was invaluable to pass the CPA license at my first try. I know that my Dad was very proud of me for being the first CPA in a family of four CPAs (my three other sisters followed in my footsteps). At the CPA firm, I worked my way up to junior partnership. I was gainfully employed and so I followed the family tradition of giving my parents my full financial support, especially since my father had retired from work at that time.

My Dad expected a lot from me since I am the oldest in the family. My siblings were still in school and he had been very vocal about his hope that I would see them through college. I accepted the responsibility as I was raised to respect my parents' wishes and grateful to them for all their hard work. I knew I had to do for my siblings what my parents did for me, as long as I was able to. There were times when I wondered what my Dad would think and say, when one day, I would tell him that I want to get married, raise a family, and move to the US. I dreaded, not if but when, that moment would come.

That time finally came in early 1977, when Conrad sent me a letter proposing that we get married in January of the following year. I could not talk him out of it. He had already made up his mind and was insisting that he would call my Dad and tell him of our plans. Actually, they were his plans because frankly, I had not completely bought into it at that point in time.

I tried to convince him that he should wait until I am able to muster enough courage to tell my Dad myself. He knew how scared I was of my Dad and believed that such a time would never come. He told me he would write my Dad instead. I thought of intercepting his letter but realized that that was not fair to him.

So I waited for his letter and prepared myself for whatever the consequences might be. Days passed, no letter came and I was apprehensive about what might happen next. I kept my silence but deep within me, I was hoping that perhaps Conrad had realized that it was not yet the proper time. Days passed, no letter came and I was apprehensive about what might happen next. I kept my silence but deep within me, I was hoping that perhaps Conrad had realized that it was not yet the proper time.

The months passed and we never talked about the wedding until that day at work in December, 1977. I received a long distance call from Hawai'i. It was Conrad letting me know that he was coming for a visit in January and insisting that we get married then. I was stunned, angry, and confused. My mind went blank and I did not know what to do next.

What scared me the most was the thought of my Dad. We ended the conversation with no definite agreement on the matter. It was up to me to think through these things. There was no one in whom to confide. I asked myself how I could possibly be fully prepared for this milestone in my life in a matter of days. How am I to decide on things when Conrad was so far away from me? How, when, and what would I say to my family about this bombshell that was about to explode? I knew time was running out. I had to decide. I was old enough to get married at 26 and even if I had not fulfilled my promise, I believed I had done my best to support my siblings in whatever way I could. In the midst of all this chaos, my Mom came to my rescue. She listened to me, gave me her blessing and the courage to face my Dad.

I remember that day when I finally told my Dad. He was in the living room with my sisters and I awkwardly walked in. I purposely wanted to have other people around, hoping they would help soften the blow, so to speak. Before I started to talk, I became teary-eyed and then I started to cry as words came out of my mouth.

"Dad I have wanted to tell you this, know that I am really afraid of you at this moment, but I must tell you Conrad and I have decided to get married." Those were the only words I could utter that very moment. I could not look directly at him as I spoke, but I could feel the disappointment on his face. He did not speak a word upon hearing what I said. Instead, he stood up and left the room. In my mind, I was thankful that he acted the way he did, because I knew I could not survive another minute in the room with him. I felt guilty for hiding things from my Dad and yet deep within, I rationalized my actions because of my fear of him. That moment I was relieved that I had finally opened up to him, but I felt a heavy heart knowing that I hurt him.

In the days that followed, my Dad never spoke to me and I decided to keep silent. That year, Christmas was uneventful for our family. I just buried myself in work, preparing for Conrad's arrival and for our wedding. I could not be more grateful to my sisters and my Mom who helped me with the errands, the phone calls, the shopping, the arrangements for the church, and the banquet. My Mom, a seamstress herself, sewed all six of my bridesmaids' gowns. Thinking about it now, I am proud that I was able to do all these by myself with Conrad coming into the picture just a few days before our wedding day.

Conrad arrived a week before our wedding. He and his family came to our house for the pamanhikan to officially ask for my parents' blessing. My Mom and my Lola Bebang (Mom's aunt) spoke to my Dad about this meeting. Conrad and his parents knew what we were up against.

Note that this was the very first time in three years that Conrad would once again see my Dad. It was a very uncomfortable circumstance. His parents were ill at ease since they had never met my parents. My Dad saw them and calmly told Conrad and his parents that he was giving us his blessing, but that he would not be attending the church wedding and the reception. That was all he had to say and left us to ourselves. I was embarrassed and apologized to Conrad's parents. They understood and I thanked them. I was devastated to hear my Dad's decision, but I respected it anyhow. My dream of a perfect wedding would never be. My childhood dream of walking down the aisle with my Dad in a wedding procession would never happen nor would I experience dancing with him at the reception. In the days that followed, I still did not lose hope that my Dad would change his mind. But as fate would have it, I would walk down the aisle with my brother Carlos and I would miss the one person that I wanted to be with on my wedding day.

Linda and Conrad through the years.

January 15, 1978, my wedding day. Our house was quiet, void of all the noise and the laughter you would expect in a house when someone is getting married that day. My Dad stayed in his room, and did not speak to me. My Mom made a last effort to convince him to come to the church, but to no avail. That very moment, I lost all hope that my Dad would soften his heart for me. Dressing up for my wedding was not exciting at all. I looked at myself in the mirror and I felt sorry for myself and realized how much I had aged in the few days that passed. Of all the days I had to be heartbroken on my wedding day. I had large pimples on my face and no make-up could conceal them. My eyes were puffy from crying the night before. I knew I would look terrible in my wedding pictures. It was the first time I had seen my wedding gown, and I knew without trying it on that it would be loose on me. I had lost weight. My Mom used safety pins to make adjustments so I could fit into the gown. I fixed my hair, using a simple head dress and wore very little make-up. The only jewelry I wore was a pair of earrings my Mom gave me. I looked so ordinary, not the bride I wanted to look like and a far cry from the princess that I had dreamed of when I was young.

Despite everything that was going through my mind and heart, I knew I had to cheer up for my groom who would be waiting for me at the altar. I grabbed my bouquet of white roses and hurried down to the black Mercedes that a friend had loaned me. Trying hard to lighten up my disposition, I told myself on the way to the church that this day will pass and it will leave me with both sad and happy memories. For now, I should put the sad memories in the back burner and look forward to the happy memories still to come.

God blessed me on that day. I married my husband Conrad at the six o'clock evening mass at Malate Church in Manila. Our families, (without my father) and friends witnessed our marriage and celebrated a milestone in our lives. It may not have been my dream wedding, but it was a blessed gift from God, a once in a lifetime experience that I will treasure. I believe my Dad was thinking of me the very moment I said "I do" and though he was not there, I knew he wished the best for me.

I felt that my Dad had softened a bit after the wedding. He warmly welcomed Conrad and me when we came back to the house. We never talked about the wedding and about our feelings with him. I am so fortunate that Conrad understood and respected him in spite of what happened. I realize that Dad stood by his words and I have never taken it against him, even after I knew years later, how differently he acted when it came to the wedding of my sisters.

Conrad had to leave for the U.S. right after our honeymoon. I stayed with my family while waiting to join Conrad in Hawai'i. He came to visit a couple of times since our wedding. I gave birth in the Philippines to my first child, Anthony. Conrad came home and spent time with my family. Perhaps the one thing that really helped us in reconciling with my Dad was my son, Anthony. As their first grandchild, he was a joy to my parents, especially to my Mom who babysat for him. I was praying that I would not hurt them again when we both had to leave for the US. In 1980, my son, Anthony and I finally joined Conrad in Hawai'i.

In 1992, my parents came to live with us in Hawai'i, but decided to settle back in the Philippines after two years. Time had healed our wounds. Although it left a scar, it no longer hurt. I felt that my Dad finally accepted that I had made the right decision then. My parents see how happy I am with my family and how my education, their legacy to me, has helped me settle down comfortably in my new home. And they are blessed with three grand children whom they love dearly. I thank God for all these blessings.

I passed every opportunity I had to ask my Dad the reasons for his decision regarding my wedding. I will never know why, at least not directly from him. Maybe If I did, I would have had a heart-to-heart talk with him. My Dad passed away in February of 2010. With his passing, I have come to realize that I will never experience that walk down the aisle with him. My golden wedding anniversary is still years from now. Silly you will say, but in my wildest imagination it is still possible, only it will be 50 years after.

Linda Abuel is a wife, mother, and grandmother. A business graduate majoring in Accounting from the University Santo Tomas in Manila, she received her CPA designation in 1972. In 1980 she moved to Hawai'i to join her husband Conrad. Her 32-year career in non-profit world started in 1984 with Child and Family Services Hawai'i. Since 2004, Linda has been the fiscal officer of the Waianae Coast Community Mental Health Center, Inc. She was the volunteer financial manager for the capital campaign to build the FILCOM Center. She held leadership positions in the Filipino Chamber of Commerce of Hawai'i, FAUW, Oahu Filipino Community Council, and other Filipino cultural organizations.

Six

RESILIENCE AND MINDFUL PRESENCE

by Edna R. Magpantay-Monroe

In April, 2011, I received a phone call from one of my sisters to tell me that my Dad had a heart attack and a stroke. I was frightened yet thinking, "How can this be possible? My Dad loves to walk every day and has never been sick too often except for a cold?" My two brothers and two sisters were together when the call was made and they asked if I could come home to Chicago. I could hear a sense of urgency and despair in their voices so I did not hesitate to oblige. I immediately told my husband the nature of the call and asked him if he can manage the household in my absence. We had a young son (nine years old at the time) with a chronic disease; he could get very sick anytime.

My husband was very supportive and agreed that I should be with my family. He quickly booked the first flight he could get for me while I packed and made my phone calls and emails to cancel any commitments I have for the next few days. Prior to leaving, I also made sure that all reminders about my son's care were posted for my husband. Luckily, during that time, I only telecommuted for work Thursday to Sunday so I could work anywhere in the world as long as I had access to good internet. I asked for a few days off from work to focus on the crisis.

I can't recall clearly the travel to Chicago, but I vividly remember how cold it was when I arrived at O'Hare airport. I think it was in the fifties! One of my younger brothers picked me up and we headed to my parent's house so I could freshen up before seeing my Dad in the hospital. My parents lived in a one-bedroom apartment where we were raised when my siblings and I joined my parents in the United States in the early 1980s. As I entered their apartment, the place looked the same as it did when I lived there. The building where my parents lived housed mostly physicians, nurses, and other healthcare workers who worked in the medical center nearby. My father worked as an accounting clerk and my mother worked as a pharmacy tech with stable companies for years. I always said that they were fortunate to have worked with companies that provided great benefits, especially after retirement.

My father was taken to one of the private hospitals in the medical center. Thank God for good insurance. It was one less thing to worry about.

I was raised to understand that family is very important. I still remember the times when we were living in my parents' one-bedroom apartment with five children. We did not have a lot of space but we had a lot of family time. The dining room table was the center of all our conversations and laughter. My Dad always had something "smart" to say about everything. One must understand his sense of humor to appreciate how he laughs and his jolliness can be contagious. The value of being with family no matter what happens has been the mantra of my life even after I got married.

The great thing is that my African-American husband of 21 years shares the same value. My only son, Donovan can understand why family is important. Our family unit is away from the extended family a lot. I am the only child living away from home; I live in Hawaiʻi, where we decided to raise our child after my husband's retirement from the United States Coast Guard. It is important for my son to know his grandparents, aunts, uncles, and cousins. We make an effort to call on special occasions and visit whenever we can.

With family gathered by his bedside at the hospital, important decisions were made about my Dad's future. All the children were assigned tasks to do. We used each other's strengths to decide who would be the power of attorney for health, who will be the power of attorney for finances, who would be responsible to talk to the doctors, who would stay at the hospital, who would take my mother home, etc. I took the coordinator role to put everything in motion. There were moments of intense feelings during the family meetings as my father had 99 percent occlusion in his heart and may not survive. My younger sister who is well connected in her place of employment found the best cardiac surgeon for our Dad.

I still remember the day of the surgery when hours of waiting seemed forever. Having to calm my mother was surreal. When my Dad returned from almost a full day of surgery, his chest remained open. This scene was probably the most traumatizing event for the family to see, especially for my mother. The surgeon explained to the family the reason for this choice but I do not believe anyone really heard him. Despite having three nurses in the family and a daughter-in-law who is a nurse, it was still a shocker for us to understand what was happening. I tried my best to help my Mom and younger sister to understand that crying in front of my Dad who was still sedated was not a good idea. I did not want my father to wake up thinking something was very wrong. I believed that my Dad could hear us even though he was heavily sedated.

This medical crisis forced all of us to pitch in despite our own responsibilities with our own families. The ability to know how to use resources effectively was key to survival. Resourcefulness is something I learned from my parents and maybe even from my inay (lola = grandmother) on my father's side. When we realized that something had to be done to get my parents in a new, safe, and comfortable environment even with limited financial resources, the children decided the course of action as part of our family responsibility.

It was quite disturbing to intervene for our parents' sake, but in the end, it was necessary. My Dad is a proud man and I

43

think this transition is something he wished his children did not have to deal with. But he was helpless. He was not the same man after the stroke, having residual weakness on the right side of his body and with limitations in his ability to speak his mind, so he couldn't object. My mother, on the other hand, insisted that it was our obligation to help our parents in return for all that they have done for us.

This notion that we are to "pay back" came quite loudly from my mother. My Dad did not seem to want all the attention and fuss. There were expectations of "thank you" that didn't happen and this resulted in resentments. Each of the siblings had his/her perception of what was expected and what would have been a nice gesture from my parents.

As a strong-willed daughter, I have learned to engage as well as set limits. I have learned to expect nothing but always do what I think is best in a situation. I often think about this situation. Having an only child, do I have the same expectations as my mother? My child often speaks about never leaving Mommy and Daddy. He also is quick to say that he will take care of us when we get older. But what is the reality?

I was amazed to see how my siblings and I helped our parents' transition into a new chapter in their lives. We moved them out of their apartment to a more supervised housing situation and closer to where my older sister lived, as requested by my Mom. We also made changes in the roles they had. Where my Dad used to care for my Mom, my Mom will now become Dad's caregiver. This was a painful reality for all.

My Dad survived open-heart surgery but the reality remains that he is a ticking time bomb. Our family knows this. Our faith, being raised Catholic, allows us to wish that he can continue to live a quality life to the very end. Hence, given medical information, my parents have decided not to consider more surgery in the near future but rather, allow God to bring His will upon my Dad. Five years after the heart attack and stroke, my Dad is determined to live the quality of life he cherishes. It has not been easy for him and my Mom. My Dad's famous phrase after the event is, "I do not know." I believe it is his way of saying life is unpredictable but I will keep on moving on.

My Dad is a Batangueño with a zest for life. Growing up, my siblings and I always saw my Dad as a serious man but he knew how to make jokes in order to make life bearable, despite the challenges and hardships. We see our Dad as a determined man who may not always show his emotions. As the daughter who majored in nursing with a focus on psychiatric mental health, I always tried to put everything that happens in some perspective. Most people who know our family believe that I inherited the zest for life from my father and his side of the family. I always seem to find something to be thankful for even under disheartening circumstances.

Last year, my Dad was diagnosed with a malignant prostate cancer. So it is just a matter of time. The family's ability to keep everything in perspective will allow us to be psychologically prepared for the inevitable. The strength of the Batangueño in my genes will allow me, as the daughter, to be ready. My mother believes that my father has the ability to survive any "bad" medical news.

My mother always believes that God provides. This is her prayer. As Catholics, we learned to go to church for all our heartaches, despair, and struggles. My mother would always tell us that we suffer because we do not PRAY! Prayer is something I always hold dear to my heart. I tell my son that his religion teacher is correct when she says that maybe not having a great relationship with God is the reason he gets "in trouble".

My parents sacrificed a good life in the Philippines for a better life and a better future in the United States. My parents value family and education. Perseverance and hard work have always been in the forefront of what they see as doing the right thing.

My parents came from two regions in the Philippines that

45

spoke two different languages—Tagalog and Ilokano. I always knew that I am a mixture of two great genetic traits: Frugality from my mother's side; and strong will from my father's side.

I also believe adaptability and resilience is written all over who I am as a person and also who we, the Magpantays, are as a family. My Dad's best advice that I have valued relates to the choices I make. He says, "If you want something real bad, you will do whatever it takes to get it. If you don't' want something real bad you will make every excuse you can find." This advice has helped me in everything I have aspired to do in life, from deciding on a career that I can cherish and be good at, to managing the challenges in my life. I have passed this advice on to my son to help him make the right choices, especially now, that he is an adolescent.

My father's medical event in 2011 brought out a characteristic in me as a Filipina that I discovered. I have used this event to understand the value of dealing with any family crises. No matter how difficult the situation was, our faith brought us together. We survived bravely and stayed as a family.

I believe that my upbringing in the Magpantay household identifies who I am—a strong and educated Filipina. I feel that I am morally obligated always to try to do my best in any situation. My "mindful presence" in any situation allows my resilience to grow strong and flourish.

When I immigrated to the United States in the early 1980s with my four siblings, I knew I wanted to be a successful Filipina. My decisions were strongly influenced by my parents. They selected a career that they thought would be best for me in order to survive. I wanted to be a doctor but my mother thought it best to be a nurse. So I chose to be a nurse. I realized later how fulfilling it can be as long as I could find my own way, i.e., that I am able to decide how and what I could choose to do to practice my profession. There were opportunities presented to me as a nurse that I believe came into fruition because of how I was brought up by my parents. For instance, they instilled in me the value of education as a key to survival. In earning a doctorate degree, I am able to give back to fellow Filipinos by sharing with them my educational journey.

I have been mindful of who I am as a Filipina since I came to this country as a college student seeking a better life. I am gratified and proud to be recognized as a Filipina. This was one of the reasons I hyphenated my name when I got married to an American. I wanted a sense of my culture and be reminded of my identity. The life events leading to my Dad's medical crisis made me realize that my strength as a person was not only in genetics, but also in environment in which I have lived most of my life. My resilience stems from several factors: My understanding of who my family is; the morals to which I adhere; the values of my own immediate family; and my aspirations in life.

Traditions have been valuable in guiding my role as a daughter, wife, mother, sibling, and aunt. Family traditions, important to my family, have also guided me in raising my only child. I think it is very meaningful to use traditions especially now, when my child is coming of age (14 years old) and growing independent. My son craves for lots of family time. The dining table is also the center of our conversations especially on weekends. Stories about what is happening in our lives as a member of the family becomes the foundation of how the family unit is working together.

In a matter of months and maybe even years, the life events that have happened will make me appreciate the gift of understanding my character. I am a Filipina who was born in Manila, raised in two places—Quezon City, Philippines and in Chicago, U.S.A. When adversities come my way, I hold on to the image of strength, humility, and faith as examples of my Filipino roots to help me navigate my way. I crave for opportunities to experience life at its fullest.

Did I ever doubt that being a Filipina in the United States, living away from the culture means giving up who I am?

I learned that if I can be mindful and reflective of who I am when I left the Philippines as a determined college student to now. Being a nurse with a doctorate degree, educating future generations of nurses, I can still be a bearer of Filipino culture. My adaptability and reliance make me a strong Filipina. Ako ay matatag dahil ako ay Filipina! I am strong because I am a Filipina!

Edna Magpantay-Monroe was born in Quezon City and immigrated to Chicago, Illinois in her late teens. She has lived in several states (Illinois, Maryland, California, and Virginia) and later decided to make Hawai'i her home. She is a nurse practicing in academia with interest in psychiatric mental health, primary care, and gerontology. She is very active in her service to the nursing profession, Filipino community, and military/veteran issues. She is married to a CWO (retired) Coast Guard and has a son.

Seven
AMPON LANG
by Rose Cruz Churma

We arrived at the Heart of Mary Villa in the middle of the day in January 1990 to pick up our daughter, Grace. After an 11-hour flight from Hawai'i, we arrived in Manila at dawn and by the time we've deposited our luggage at my brother's house, I was ready to go and see her.

"Can't we wait until tomorrow?" my husband Tom pleaded. He could not sleep during the entire flight.

I was insistent. We waited too long for this. After five years from the time we decided to adopt, we were finally meeting our daughter Grace. All we had was a photograph of her at a few weeks after birth—her brown eyes directly looking at the camera and her curly hair framing her face like a dark halo. It was all we had the last 10 months as we waited for the bureaucratic paperwork of the countries on either side of the Pacific to allow us to bring her to Hawai'i.

My siblings were supportive. My parents on the other hand, particularly my mom, had very mixed feelings.

From the get-go, my mom was adamant that we should adopt a baby related to us by blood. She wanted us to adopt a niece, the daughter of one of my brothers who had the most kids but the least resources.

"We'll put you on the stand," a sibling who is a lawyer explained to my mom, "and you will be forced to testify that your son is an unfit parent," my brother warned her. This was the only way the Philippines and the USA will allow a relative adoption for a non-orphan—that either or both parents were

49

unfit.

In Hawai'i, the social service agency that processed our adoption had only dealt with "relative adoptions" from the Philippines. It was more common, according to the social workers. Filipinos were more inclined to adopt relatives. We would be the first at Child and Family Service to adopt a "non-related" Filipino baby.

Rose meets baby Grace.

We started the process in 1987 when Corazon Aquino was catapulted into the Philippine presidency after a "people power" revolution. The head of the social services department in Aquino's cabinet only allowed the adoption of Filipino babies overseas to Filipino couples, or at least to couples where one of the prospective parent is Filipino. Thankfully, we qualified.

When we arrived at the Heart of Mary Villa, we were directed to a one-story building made of concrete hollow blocks. The nursery, as it was referred to, had rows and rows of cribs all occupied by infants. Strangely, for a room filled with babies, the place was quiet—no screaming babies but the calm and soothing voice of a nun who was obviously in charge of the place. A cloud of baby powder enveloped the front of the room. On a changing table lay a curly-haired baby just wearing diapers.

"It will be Christmas every day now," the nun crooned at the baby. "Your parents are here to bring you home." The nun took the pink dress I offered as we came in. When we had called earlier to let them know that we were coming, she had requested that we bring clothes for our daughter.

"I want to pick her up first," Tom said as he elbowed me away. Earlier, during the long car ride from Makati to Malabon, he nodded off due to jet lag and had pleaded to postpone the trip to Malabon for one more day. Obviously the adrenalin had kicked into his system. He scooped up Grace in his arms and danced around the room. Grace hugged his neck but she eyed me quietly—her eyes following me.

"My turn, my turn!" I said. I couldn't wait to hold her. Finally I hugged her close to me. Interestingly throughout the entire time, Grace remained quiet, but her eyes spoke volumes especially when Tom picked up the other baby girl next to Grace's crib. Her eyes seemed to say, "Why are you holding that baby?" Tom would say that Grace gave Bernadette the stink eye. A couple from Belgium was adopting Bernadette. And just like in Grace's case, the paperwork took a while. In the entire nursery, these two babies were the oldest, almost a year old, due to the delays in processing their papers for a home overseas.

During the first few days, Grace was so unnaturally quiet. Most of the time, she had her two fingers stuck to her mouth, and would remove it only when she was sucking her bottle. "Is there something wrong with her?" I asked my sister. The first night, she didn't cry at all. We watched her sleep and pulled the two fingers from her mouth once she fell into a deep sleep, but the moment she woke up, she would utter a short yelp and then suck her fingers and look at you with those expressive eyes. "Give it some time," my sister said. "In the orphanage, there were so many babies, nobody came when she cried. Once she realizes that you are there, she'll cry now to get your attention," my sister said.

Sure enough, after a few days, she acted more normally, crying when she was hungry or wet. But unlike some babies, she would cheerfully allow most of the adults around to pick her up, and bestow on them one of her beautiful smiles.

During those first few days, we stayed at my brother's house. Whenever Tom picked her up, he noticed that the domestic helpers would relieve him of Grace. "Why are they taking her away from me every time I pick her up?" he asked me, puzzled.

"They believe that child care is a woman's role," I explained. It took some explaining to the well-meaning household help that Tom wanted to be hands-on in taking care of his daughter. After that, they cheerfully included Tom in the impromptu workshops we had on childcare.

Our next hurdle was to bring her to meet my parents who lived in Baguio. Knowing my mom's disappointment that we still proceeded with this adoption despite her concerns made me wary about bringing Grace there. But all my siblings felt that it was the proper thing to do—to introduce our daughter to her grandparents no matter what reaction we would receive.

At that time, Philippine Airlines still flew to Baguio. The flight attendants took turns holding her, and Grace responded with her smile. As we descended the plane at the tarmac, I caught a glimpse of my parents waiting for us, with the rest of their Baguio-based grand children.

52

"Here goes, Tom," I said. "Let us hope this will be painless." My mom is known to speak her mind, and after a grueling five-year process of adoption, I was not ready for another round of pessimism about how adopted children bring you heartaches and headaches. Isn't that true of most children, adopted or not?

We would surmise later that perhaps Grace knew the one person she should charm first. The moment we got close to where my parents waited, she stretched her small arms to my mom, her smile pleading to be picked up. My mom picked her up and Grace wrapped her arms around her neck and nestled her head on her shoulder. The look on my mom's face was priceless—something I will always remember. From that point on, there was no more talk about the problems of adopting children with unknown backgrounds or the problems of bringing up children with strange bloodlines.

I always believed that whether it is via adoption or natural birth, one can never predict the child's personality or how he/she will turn out to be as adults. There's the nurture versus nature argument, but in the end, it's like the roll of the dice. You never know what you'll get, or how the child will turn out someday.

But I understood my mom's concerns. During the Japanese occupation, my maternal grandparents adopted a little boy barely two years old. It was a time of turmoil and upheaval, so in essence the adoption process was informal. In a transaction in front of my grandfather's farmacia, my grandmother took the toddler in her arms and brought him home. She had lost a baby when they evacuated to the countryside after the fall of Bataan. So the little boy became the bunso (youngest) of the family.

Despite the fact that my grandmother adopted my uncle in an informal way, she kept the clothes that he wore when he went home with her. In the same way I still keep Grace's adoption documents in a safe and secure place. My grandmother kept my uncles things, lovingly encased in indestructible plastic and stowed in a secret compartment of her aparador. When she was widowed in her seventies, she showed me her important keepsakes. The case containing his clothes was one of them—a brown, short overalls with metal buttons, caked with dirt, a silent testimony to a life-altering decision made years ago.

In those days, adoptions were kept a secret, at least that was my perception. I spent summers at my grandparents' house and the adoption was never discussed openly, but at five years old, I knew about it. The domestic help talked about it in whispers, especially when my uncle got into some teen-aged misadventures. "Ampon lang kasi (because he's only adopted)," they would say. One incident was particularly vivid in my memory. My grandparents and my uncle were huddled in the kitchen in the middle of the afternoon with raised voices. My uncle was crying and through his anguished sobs he was telling them an incident that happened earlier that day. Apparently he had gone to one of his classmates' house to ask her father's permission to escort her to the school dance. He was rudely asked to leave. "Ampon ka lang!" the girl's father said. It was at that time that my uncle realized he was adopted. It was an open secret in town, where everybody knew except him.

So when we adopted Grace, the nuns at the orphanage were very insistent on making sure we openly discussed this with her. Her favorite bedtime story was when we came to Heart of Mary Villa to pick her up, and how her Auntie Janice met us at the airport, and how her Grandma Mary and Grandpa George came all the way from Florida to welcome her in Hawai'i. She was lovingly welcomed by Tom's family and by our friends.

Despite this openness, it is difficult to know at what age she could grasp the concept. One time when she was four, we were both watching a TV sitcom where the main character was shown giving birth in a hospital room. "Is that how I came out of your tummy?" Grace asked. "No," I said. "You came out of another mommy's tummy. I am the mommy who takes care of you." I replied calmly. I thought that was the end of the discussion. But several days later, she handed me a beautiful valentine card that she had been working on. "This is for the mommy who had me in her tummy. Can we send this to her?" My heart dropped to my toes as I accepted the card. "Of course," I said. And I did, sending it to the orphanage with a letter to the nuns and giving them an update on how Grace was doing.

When she was about six, a delegation of her neighborhood friends trooped over to the kitchen while I was washing dishes. The most assertive girl stepped up to the front of the line and asked me, "Where is Grace's real mom?" I noticed Grace at the periphery of the group, with a perplexed look on her face. Several pairs of eyes were focused on me. During times like these when you get asked earth-shaking questions, you always wonder if you said the right thing. "I am her real mom," I said. "Am I not real enough? Can't you see me, Can't you hear me?" Grace seemed happy enough with my answer at that time, but each growing-up phase carried its own challenges.

When she was in middle school, she casually asked us if we could stop going to her school. Then she modified it somewhat. "Maybe Mom can go, but not you Dad. The kids ask too many questions, and I am tired of explaining why my Dad is so haole, but I look this way—and she tossed her jet black hair, and pointed to her skin, the color of coffee with just a hint of milk.

That phase fizzled fast when her dad volunteered to be the girls' volunteer "assistant-to-the-assistant" basketball coach. Grace was not part of the team but attended the practices and games and observed the rapport her dad had with her peers. If her classmates thought he was okay, then he must be, she reasoned.

"Dad, I must have inherited your left-handedness and your curly hair," she observed soon after. That was the end of that issue, and the beginning of new ones.

When we decided to adopt, I bought a painting titled "Hanai." It still hangs in the living room and in moments when parenthood, and now grandparenthood, drags me down with demands on my time and my patience, I am grateful that Hawai'i is now my home. Hanai is a Hawaiian cultural practice where a child is brought into another's household and brought up as their own. It implies the act of offering a precious gift—one's child—rather than giving a baby away. Now, the word hanai is loosely used to include any form of informal adoption. It does not however, have the negative connotation that "ampon" has in the Filipino language, usually expressed as "ampon lang," giving the adoptee a second-class status versus the natural-born siblings. When we visit the Philippines, I am very sensitive to that perception, and my hackles rise whenever any comments are made that would make my daughter feel less than she should. Thankfully, my siblings and extended family have been very supportive. Other cousins have chosen the path I took, and we are grateful that our daughters have been accepted wholly and fully.

But still, I cringe whenever someone thoughtlessly comments "ampon lang iyan."

Several weeks ago, the oldest son of my adoptive uncle called to ask: "I'll be in Hawai'i soon. Can we meet?"

We met for lunch at a Filipino restaurant in Waipahu and, over familiar dishes of pinakbet and papaitan, he told me that my uncle had passed away. "My regret is that he shared very little of the past with us," my cousin said. "Whenever we asked, he would change the subject."

So I shared with him what I can remember, and mourned the fact that my grandparents' ancestral home has since been dismantled when the Pinatubo eruption covered it with lahar, and very few of its contents survived.

There is a Filipino saying—"hindi ka makakarating sa iyong pupuntahan kung hindi ka lumilingon sa iyong pinangalingan"—translated loosely as "you will not reach your destination if you don't acknowledge where you came from." Perhaps it is a universal human trait to seek one's roots; it is not unique to Filipino culture. But this is one trait I unconsciously shared with my daughter. I also understood why it was important for my cousin to search for his father's past.

It was not a surprise to me that at 18, my daughter asked my help in searching for her biological mother. "Some don't want to be found," I warned her. As a mother, it is hard to ignore one's protective instincts. The nuns at the orphanage offered to do what they could, but as the years went by without any word from them, the search decreased as a topic to be discussed or pursued. Still, when we visited Manila some time ago, she pointed at the urban shanties that we passed by and asked if we can explore the area. "Maybe we can find my mom there," she said.

We took the advice of the nuns to heart—we had shared all that what we knew, and she had deduced that poverty must have been one of the reasons why she was given up for adoption. So she looked wistfully at every squatter area we passed by, any brown face with the same curly hair at the marketplace or the mall. I can sense the questions going through her mind, but I was helpless to provide any answers.

One of the reasons the Philippine government insisted that at least one of the adoptive parents should be Filipino is to ensure that the adoptive child grows up knowing her cultural heritage. But Grace also cherished her adoptive father's French-Canadian-Irish-Slovak heritage. Her mainland-based grandparents never missed important landmarks in her childhood and Grace spent countless hours with her dad's sister who chose to live in Hawai`i. Last year, against my better judgment, she drove from Chicago to Lansing, Michigan during the middle of winter. "I made angels in the snow," she said.

"Just like Dad did when he was a boy, in the same park where he played ball." She described the house where her Dad's family lived and chuckled that the current neighbors thought she must be a stalker as she drove around the block several times.

Adoption is not for the faint of heart—for the adoptee, nor the adoptive parents. Still if I were to do it all over again, I would, and pray that I can offer enough love to make it easier on my daughter and her children to seek and accept the past, just like what my cousin has decided to do. More importantly, it is imperative to move on and create new memories and traditions to pass on to the next generation.

Since moving to Hawai'i in 1976, Rose served in various capacities from file clerk to math teacher, political cartoonist to project manager to administrator for non-profit and government organizations. In 1987, she established DesignLab, architecture and planning firm that completed over a hundred projects locally, the US Mainland, the Philippines and other Pacific Island nations. She also co-owns an online bookstore, Kalamansi Books & Things that specializes in Filipiniana publications. She and her husband live in Kaneohe and have a daughter and two grandsons.

Eight
A MOTHER'S STORY: BETWEEN THREE COUNTRIES

by Maya Jezewski

Flipinen! Filipinen! Those sounds buzzed in my brain as our train entered Poland.

I didn't quite see what was happening or what was to come. That was 1975 and we were entering by a crack on the Iron Curtain. My fiancé and I had our minds full of a wedding in Warsaw, and nothing else mattered...thus starts this mother's story.

How did she find herself in this situation? Her life now revolves around three persons—husband, two children—and three countries (husband's Poland, children's France, and her very own Philippines). My story began earlier, much earlier. Martial law in the Philippines...

I had to leave the country in a hurry, for my parents, my mentors, those who cared urged me to leave the country I just began to really know. For their peace of mind, I boarded a spaceship to a distant planet from which I'd never return.

I landed in England, then France, and met but measly humans. Aah, how to relate? With a straight back, my head so high it could scrape the sky, I watched. So, they like us quiet, un-opinioned, apathetic, lower the head a few degrees down, watch the white natives from the corner of an eye, invisible, spontaneity held in check, my innate curiosity camouflaged the himantayun (nosiness), the bugal-bugalun (mocking)! I'd coil, lean back, lie low, like a snake before striking.

59

Polish-Filipino: Christophe, Adam, Maya, Mayumi and her partner Thomas, and baby Eva in a Paris suburb.

With the hollow in my solar plexus, I queried, queried. How to cry for help in another tongue? How to forget Mama's abhorrence for indebtedness, material or moral, that overpowering pride in self-sufficiency, that innate distrust of strangers, so friendly, so wary.

How Did I Find My Life Partner?

Well, actually, he found me. He was sure, he said, he'd find me. As I studied French at the Alliance Française in Paris, he looked for me. Finally a compatriot would introduce us. My internal dislike for that meeting quickly vanished when, on his face, I saw the call of destiny?

My shyness, prudishness, and suspicious character slowly melted like snow in spring. Perhaps we were meant to keep each other company, each day for another, as we chatted long hours, on the promenades at the Luxembourg gardens, listening to classical music in his little room under the roof, holding hands in theatres, at the Opera. As time would stop with each encounter, we didn't feel the fast vehicle under our feet, nothing but a throb of eternity. Is time a particle of destiny? Soon he was calling his mom in Warsaw, who quickly jumped on the first plane to Paris to meet me, officially, but more especially to make sure that her only son hadn't lost his mind!

My husband, partner in life in education, child-rearing— his universe, I embraced. The day we took the train to Poland, I didn't fully realize what it meant to go behind that fearsome Iron Curtain. Mama-in-law was a very elegant lady who could rub elbows with any European aristocrat, her intelligence equal if not superior to most professionals in the West. My fiancé had nothing of a Soviet communist, but a fervent Catholic like most Poles, tutored by a French governess till the Soviets expelled her with other compatriots. His being had nothing of my limited idea of citizens in a Communist country. My mind in tabula rasa took that train to Poland...

So, dreamily, I looked up to the sky, perusing its luminous blue, when that same sky groaned in an instant's solar eclipse! Or so it seemed, for as soon as we moved out of West Berlin to enter East Germany, I felt the gloom descend from heaven, or did it rise from earth's bowels?! The sudden hush, the muffled sounds, the tension, the pallor, the terrorized look in faces with the heavy entry of East German border patrolers, harshness carved on each face, flashlights like lethal weapons, their growling German shepherds.

I sank heavily into my train seat. Passport/identity controllers would follow, their cold breath chilling many a heart with their irritable snappy voices. Did our train suddenly swerve into the dark side of the moon? Did we turn into little green men, lost in space? I gripped my fiancé's arm, held my breath, for my turn would surely come to freeze under those terrible Medusa eyes! When suddenly, a miracle!

"Filipinen," his hard discipline melting as he asked kindly, "Do you want your visa on a separate sheet? I think your passport forbids you to travel to Communist countries." In shock, I quietly nodded, not daring to say, "You're wrong. We are now allowed." By then, he had already passed my passport on to another controller who in turn passed it on to another…and I could hear over the length of the train corridor their excitement, Filipinen! Filipinen! Quite obviously, I was the first Filipina to come that way.

Our Common World

Many an outsider's knowledge of Poland is limited to: It's communist, isn't it? The Poles are anti-Semitic, aren't they? One of their female athletes was actually a man, wasn't he or was he a she?

This great country gave birth to Copernicus, Chopin, Joseph Conrad, Mickiewicz, Norwid, Marie Sklodowsaka-Curie, Wajda, Szymanowksi, Koszcuiszkio, Pulaski, Pilsudski, Malinowski, Paderewski, Rubinstein, Milosz, Pope Jean-Paul II, to name a few in the endless list of illustrious personalities who brought knowledge, light, beauty, and value to humanity—these people often known through silly little stories, over-charged with disinformation. I myself was surprised to learn that in the 14th century, Poland was Polin (meaning, here you should dwell) for the Jews, their name for the only European country that opened its doors to them when they suffered persecution and expulsion from all over Europe, starting with England. The majority of Jews had settled in Poland by WWII, so anti-Semitism incarnate grim reaper Hitler had a good harvest!

Poland and the Philippines, I discovered, have many things in common. Both countries, which sit next to each other in international conferences, are in majority Catholic. Manila and Warsaw were the most devastated capitals in WWII. They both had the misfortune of having to deal with Spain. As rumor has it, King Philip, after whom the Philippines was named, hired a killer to get rid of a Polish queen (of Italian origin) to whom he owed a large sum of money, which to this day is unpaid. My husband sadly adds, "You and I also share political solitude, the absence of sincere allies."

On the brighter side, Polish people are commonly bright, affectionate, sentimental, hospitable. Polish nobility is quite akin to old middle class families in the Philippines, with similar traditions and way of life. I should have met your parents and asked for your hand. For us, it's the proper way, my Ma-in-law once whispered. It's our way too, I whispered back.

Alas, the Philippines has suffered from the gradual loss of ancestral oral traditions, our historical and epic memory eclipsed, our slow progress with the written word, our dying memory in the series of brain transplants since 1521, those alien conquerors from far away, their way of thinking in opposition (they could have come from Mars)! From centuries of battering and re-molding our psyche, are we now re-molding to overcome age-old handicaps. We're getting there, digging into our past, renewing nature, indigenous trees and plants, healing herbs, healing people.

Ah, to resurrect a true Philippine soul which is neither East nor West, neither Capitalist nor Communist, neither Left nor Right, I sighed while watching my children grow, but just human in the most noble sense of the word, with our own resources, nourished by clear sea waters, the warm volcanic soil, touching wisdom from Philippine undergrounds, listening to

63

the elements.

After the civil rites at the Wedding Palace in Warsaw's Old Town, the offering of my bouquet at my husband's baptismal church, our bonding, we went back to Paris to build our familial nest and continue our French adventure. France is a good midway country, between Poland and the Philippines. Civilized enough, open enough, culturally enriched with a great social security system and efficient public transport system, enough multi-ethnicity to provide fresh air, and, especially for the children, far from the prying eyes of an over-protective extended family. The family could live and develop, our intimacy unhindered. By then, I was ready to re-discover France and Europe in the context of a mixed marriage, or the Philippines in light of my union with a Polish poet.

Children Came, Unexpectedly, But Desired

How could I imagine myself without offspring? But, they came unprogrammed. I never used contraceptive means, thinking that if a child had to come, he or she would, and yet, each one came like off-season fruit, surprising, special, and precious.

It may take two to tango, but it takes much more to raise a child. It's a whole universe that's often lost in mist by stroke of conceit. Quite often, we end up humiliated, helpless before our terrible ignorance. A Filipina mother's Catholic conscience is pockmarked with damaging guilt feelings.

How to bring them up in migrant solitude? Dr. Spock helped, but my only really powerful guide was the memory of my parents and of my family in Cebu.

My Papa and Mama probably had the same anxieties. But being at home in Cebu with models in their past or present, in their natural environment, it must have been less complicated, or was it?

My (Model) Family in Cebu

Besides absolute rules, respect of elders, (including older

sisters and brothers), age-old rituals like Amin at sundown, there were rules of hospitality, and of gratitude when I was growing up in Cebu.

Animistic traditions seeped in through grandparents and aunties: Respect or perish! With all beings, visible and invisible, be humble. Before trees or lakes that are home to the dili ingun natu (spirits), be humble. Respect! Don't hurt the unseen by throwing things out of the window at night. Say "tabi" when with OFWs from Paris, who give food and drinks to Sto. Niño.

Home rules were pretty strict. Morning greetings, with a smile to start the day. Breakfast at seven, lunch at 12, and supper at six (or was it seven?)—everyone came home for meals. Meals were sacred as Holy Mass. Nothing rude, vulgar nor tragic in conversations, nothing to upset digestion, and no money on the dining table as they ate, rules etched in the family neuron. Off meals, as youngsters, we were just ordinary fun-loving kids, playing traditional games like shiatung, bituk-bituk, or buwan-buwan with parents on a full moon, loving those visits to Kayam, San Remigio, Bantayan Island, that blind man who told ghost stories on our cousin's terrace.

Papa, the family sage, knew how to listen and counsel, humbly. He taught us respect. His mantra: "Aw, iya ra sad na"—meaning, well, that's the way he is; just let him be. He wasn't saying "it's none of our business." For him, it's our business to respect another person's way of being. Let him be, as long as he doesn't have malicious intent—iya ra sad na!

Mama is the typical hard-working, self-sacrificing woman, with high pain tolerance. This is something she passed on to her daughters, as I did to my daughter, who's probably passing it on to hers. Mama, an artist, a creative mind with such clever hands, passed her talents on to the next generations. Molded the traditional way, learning domestic art and task, she opted for additional (university) knowledge, which made her a formidable adversary in home debates. For a mother, charged with the care of another life, cogitation, and creativity intensifies.

Child-rearing

I never regretted saying yes to Mama's request never to entrust my babies to baby sitters, despite the financial problems it entailed. It wasn't that much of a sacrifice since I never had pressing ambitions; I'd take what life offered, with gratitude. I can't say it was painless, but then again, what's painless in anything worth doing, or being? It was a question of priority and my children were top of the list. Husband came next, for we were partners in the enterprise. He had to participate in everything that concerned the children's welfare as well as with household matters. Although a poet is quite often on the moon and getting him down to earth is more difficult than picking a distant guava with a short stick.

From their first day of birth till their first days in school, I stayed with our children. Babies had their beds in our room at night (or I couldn't sleep), our presence in the dark their constant lullaby.

You can't regret what enriches. When you agree to sacrifice something, it's always for something better. During the day, house chores done, my children asleep, I'd draw, paint or write, next to their beds. From sociologist, I became mother, painter, writer, teacher, and thanks to my children, other dimensions opened up to me.

One day, I asked my children to please re-instate in their vocabulary the word sacrifice! They were growing up the French way and the French seem to find the term embarrassing. Often, I had to insist on my way.

"Don't give me that I-don't-care look!" I'd say. "I know you'll do as you like, but let me talk. It's my job! I'm your mother." Both of us, as parents, had to set house rules, regarding language (proper), comportment at home and outside (proper), which were generally respected—generally.

How to protect my children? What's healthy, what's toxic in their food, on TV, in their toys, the books they read? How to keep hem sturdy, to keep the balance between pain and pleasure? I learned some strategies. Kids must enjoy their food for good digestion, and consumption. So, if they're picky, be tricky! Vegetables camouflaged in their favorite spaghetti, in their burgers.

"Why were we such healthy children, Ma?" asked my daughter. Hmmm. Was it perhaps my constant presence and counsel? Inventiveness in feeding? Isn't food a blessing? Spending time to analyze their habits, their preferences, their needs? Was it because I tried to learn alternative medicine, medicinal herbs? Was it the massage, the healing techniques I picked up from practitioners? Was it those sleepless nights, when they were sick, keeping watch, caressing their brow, their head, their arms, wiping fever away? What is the secret of health?

Adolescence changed quite a few things, the children less communicative, fearing disapproval, maybe? Wanting their margin of freedom? I, who used to be their all, their absolute mama, little by little became "Filipina," or so their adolescent eyes preferred to see when the going got rough. Statements like, "Why don't you just sleep when we're out, like French mothers do?" or "You are not in the Philippines anymore, Ma," came out frequently.

Our weakness and shortcomings became more and more visible to our children, and to ourselves, through their eyes. Were we so lacking as parents? Did they worry about that fearsome breaking point? They became mirrors of our less glorious selves.

This critical part of their young lives became critical for us too, as we had to face reality in those truthful eyes. Their father had a more difficult time. My social activism was a good school for criticism and self-criticism. Their questions were many and their impatience great when the answers came slowly, small exchanges could turn into violent debates. We tried to develop competence; their minds worked at an amazing speed as they grew, in inverse proportion to ours.

Slowly, and through their own efforts in reaching maturity, my children began to understand, learned to forgive. Gone was the great violence when father and children talked or argued. Now they enjoy and laugh together, knowing their father, admiring his mind, his literary being, and his passion. They themselves grew up to be passionate artists, taking pride in being half-Polish, half-Philippine. Their two-rooted origins became their strength. Those genes, those memories, make up my children's heritage. My son likes to quote a TV series: A tree with two roots is stronger, more powerful.

When our daughter, in her twenties, says, "Mama, when I have children of my own, I'll bring them up the way you brought us up, the Philippine way," it's not only nice to hear. It's miraculous! Considering the enormous job of being a Filipina mom in France, of agonizing moments, of doubting my ability to parent, assisted only by memory. Not to mention that now-and-then feeling of disapproval from my own flesh and blood when they began to shed their children's clothing to choose their own, the start of their personal struggles towards independence.

When my young adult son suddenly blurted out one day, "Ma, we must thank you for teaching us the art of happiness," I couldn't believe my ears! Can you repeat, son? I asked twice. Was he just particularly happy that day? But then, again, I'd like to think that somewhere, somehow, I must have done something right during those years of battling to realize my own idea of an effective mother, peering at my children's faces for traces of my limitations and failures or the brightness of their souls. Those years were not lost.

At one point, I asked my son's opinions on a friend who turned bad. What makes the difference, son? The answer was quick:

Parents. It's the parents, Ma.

 *In Paris they call her by her pen name Maya. She says: "Schooled in Cebu City and Manila, the best part of me is Philippine, Noval to be precise. Once sociologist, I'm now mostly writer and painter. My poet-husband, Christophe, with his fascinating Poland, adds another dimension in life; we have artist-children Adam and Mayumi. Eva, our first apo, is my happy reason to say…France, merci!"*

SPIRIT WORLDS
&
ANCIENT WISDOMS

Duli snake bone headdress from the Cordillera.

Nine
ILI, BIAG, DAGA
by Grace Caligtan

Bound across generations, women in the Philippines and in the diaspora have all been impacted by colonization, occupation, and war. We can find healing, however, in the resilient story of birth and the creative power to nurture our body/mind/spirit and the land we walk on and share. In the following, I weave and meditate on my ancestors' story and my own story during the pregnancy and birth process of my child, Malaya Phoung Caligtan-Tran.

As a form of atang (ritual offering), I share it with you here. Threading together a set of Cordillera values centered on community, life, and land, I foreground these stories to honor birth as a powerful rite of passage. It is not simply a potential medical emergency or single hospital event to be managed. Birth serves as portal to a time continuum that allows us to reclaim the wisdom and resilience of those who have gone before. I only ask permission to cross the landscape of (y)our imagination. Let us learn to see ourselves outside of our conditioning. Bari, bari, Apo. Please excuse me, ancestors and spirits, if I offend you. Bari, bari, Apo.

Ili (Village, Community)

The Kankaney Igorot[1], and Ilokana lolas in my family have a lineage of giving and attending to women in birth during times of duress, occupation, and war. My paternal grandmother, Marcelina Ticad Dominguez, was born inside of Camp John Hay in 1915. She trained as a rural public health nurse at Baguio General Hospital and she was one of the first to return to her ili (village) to open a public health clinic in her father's home in Poblacion-Tadian, Mountain Province. She was among the first to teach me about strength and survival.

In many more ways, through her three unconventional marriages in the 1940s through World War II and the post-war years, I learned that love and partnership could exist outside of the narrow parameters of what had been offered through Catholic teachings about sin, sex, and gender roles. From her, I learned contradictions between the idea of paganism and living in Christian manner that could be confused and blurred. And lastly, I learned through her tough personal choices, that one could take responsibility for one's own happiness.

After disappointing earlier unions with two previous partners who seemed to not understand her unique position as a native woman with an education and training to serve her community, Lola Mary set out on her own to do what she needed to do. With three children in tow, she asked for her father's support to build her own home near the i-Tadian's papatayan, the clinic, and the Elementary School. The papatayan is the traditional offering table around which the i-Tadian hold their begnas and make their offerings. It still stands there today and is a reminder, perhaps, one does not live life

---

[1] Cordillera Peoples: This is the indigenous population of the Cordillera mountain range, which covers six provinces in the middle of Northern Luzon – Abra, Apayao, Benguet, Ifugao, Kalinga, and Mountain Province. The people are collectively called **Igorots**, meaning "mountain people," although some groups like the Kalingas and Ifugaos refuse to be called Igorots except by their own tribes. There are eight ethno-linguistic groups in the Cordillera, namely, Bontoc, Ibaloi, Ifugao, Isneg, Kalinga, Kankanaey, Tingguian, and Yapayao.

without a certain sacrifice.

In the process of building this home, Lola Mary fell in love again for the third time with a man from Sabangan who helped build her new house in the poblacion. The elder's joke—that it was very difficult for him to leave her cooking. Today, this house still stands and if you look out the kitchen window, you will see her buried on her land next to the man she says could make her smile and laugh, in the place where she raised her children and where she blended her family with her husband's.

To some she may have been characterized as a woman who lived ahead of her time. To others, however, who understand more deeply the context of how Igorot trial marriages and the olag/ulog (the sleeping house) worked and the way globalization influences the soul and psyche, she was someone who brought forward tradition while breaking with it simultaneously. Beyond ideas of counter-culture "free love" or western mainstream feminist notions of independence, I would like to believe that my Lola Mary embodied a different kind of personal sovereignty through her every day loves and life—the same kind of personal sovereignty that ultimately vests authority and accountability with a direct relationship with Apo Kabunian (Creator) and the reciprocal care of daga (the land), itself. It is an autonomy that I believe where all women as co-creators get to make choices that are right for their bodies and for the full context of their lives.

Though my Lola's context and my own differ across time and space, I quickly found out, in all sorts of ways, that being pregnant at 28, just barely out of graduate school, living with my partner, and not married still carried a stigma. Here I was in the year 2000, a grown woman, and I thought it was not at all out of the norm to choose to have a child outside of the bonds of the institution of marriage. Instead I had to navigate a great deal of social pressure. Ultimately, my partner and I chose to craft agreements and design a commitment ceremony that honored our mutual wishes for a loving partnership that honored a high degree of personal freedom, while taking seriously our new role as parents and our responsibilities to the place where we would raise our child. Though Lola was already in a declining state with dementia by the time I was ready to have my baby, it was her story that I looked to for guidance. It is her spirit I look to today, that serves as a template not only for me, but also for Malaya and those who will become our future ancestors.

BIAG (Wellspring of Life)

My mother's nickname is Warlina, given during a time when her family was forced to hide from Japanese soldiers in the Ilocos Norte rice fields. Warlina or Emma went on to become an OB-GYN resident at Grace Hospital in Detroit, giving birth to me the day after the last day of her OB residency. She went on for a second residency in Anesthesia. This training was quite a privilege and a challenge for my mother at the time, serving as the only female foreign medical graduate in a class of all men. In the 1970s, she was a pioneer.

As you probably can guess, the conditions of her western techno-scientific medical training probably did not make her a fan of unmediated or natural physiologic birth. Though, perhaps, I know her early experiences as a young woman witnessing her aunt die in child-birth also must have informed this, leading her to believe that OB training was the next logical step—a way in her mind, to make birth "safer, monitored, and controlled."

So in 2000, when it was time to deliver my first and only child, I was sternly told that I was a big woman and would be unable to give birth naturally. Based upon protocols dealing with gestational diabetes and hypertension that bigger women have, my mother was attendant to the statistical risks and the potential harm that could happen. She urged me to go to the hospital right away though I was in early labor. It took my doula and husband teaming up to protect the space, to stop taking her calls, and to allow me to do what I needed to do in the comfort of my own home.

Though well intended, my mother was not paying attention to the reality that over nine months, I had a healthy and supported pregnancy and absolutely none of the signs. Her anxiety, past trauma, and fear were her filter, but I could not let her training stop me or be the determiner of my actions. For the sake of honoring and respecting ancestral birth wisdom that was larger than either of us, this birth story had to be different. I had to find a way to honor the oxytocin or love hormone that flows through all of us to help us bond instead of using the adrenaline and cortisol that make us afraid and make us want to fight or run away. Too much fear had run our physiologies and nervous systems in the past.

As planned, we later went to Queens Hospital when heavy labor began. I was checked in at six centimeters. My doula, best friend, and husband set up a birthing tub for comfort. I labored there in a variety of non-supine positions— in and out of the tub, without medication, standing and squatting in the shower. The nursing team was great in allowing intermittent monitoring. It was extremely tempting during transition to take the path that would ease the sharp pains. Back labor was strong. But my doula's soft singing in my ear and her earnest words, "Every woman goes through this," kept me in my breath and breathing deep down under my piko (belly button).

In the background of the hospital room, I saw the headdress of snake bones or duli that are intended to protect a woman in childbirth and the tapis weaving my grandmother had made, carefully hung. This tapis had been at my college graduation and it was here to weave and hold this new life coming forward. Moaning on my hands and knees, I remembered my Kankaney grandmother's stories and sacrifice, so that every surge and every deep guttural utterance became like a primal birth chant honoring every women in my lineage who had come before me.

I remember closing my eyes, completely submerging under water, and just allowing the surges to come over me. Together with this strong female guardian presence, I finally surrendered to the waves of surges and just became nothing, crossing a very important bridge and rite of passage that I believe natural birth allows. Fifteen hours later from the onset of the first contractions, I gave birth to my daughter with very minor tears and was able to breastfeed and go skin-to-skin with her right away. My partner cut the cord and the placenta was respectfully placed in a container without any question or hesitation. The golden hour, or the time of the great bonding, occurred with very little interruption though still in the hospital. "Remember you are and were her first home" were the words my doula left me with. Present at my birth and around my birth were five critical elements that I believe ensures good outcomes and helps foster high satisfaction with my childbirth experience. These elements are what I also try to provide as a birth doula and what I endeavor to uphold as a midwife apprentice. In the language of evidence-based maternity care, I had:

1) Continuous skilled labor support-before, during, and after;

2) Non invasive forms of pain relief with the immersion of water and massage;

3) Support and freedom to take a variety of positions from hands and knees to hip opening squatting;

4) Early skin-to-skin contact;

5) Support with breast-feeding and allowing the baby to room in, and latch at her own pace.

But within that narrow language something is missing—a certain quality of ancestral wisdom that I'm not even sure I have all the complete words or understanding for. This "something" that one can call an ancestral bond is also the intentional ability to co-create for the mother/child pair. Birth allows the primal force of the mother's body to re-story deep

76

rooted trauma and pain. This "something," this quality of being able to allow a mother this rite of passage in her own layered cultural contexts, is what I want to bring forward and highlight. For me, it is encoded in Kankaney cultural symbol of the duli or the snake bone head-dress and the overall Cordillera mountain practice of the burial of our placenta, which is a practice shared through the Austronesian Pacific and Hawai'i. It is also "something" that can be severed and easily disregarded in a medical setting when there can be very little cultural respect and cultural humility around a birthing mother. My history, my grandmother's history, my mother's history—these things cannot be held by the medical institution. They can only be cradled deeply by the land.

Daga (Land)

"Behold the breasts that fed you, the mountains that gave you life. Destroy us, and you destroy yourselves." – *Attributed to an anonymous defender of the Chico River*

"Our forefathers have said it before, and I will also say now: Of what use and good would gold be to us when it means destroying our rice fields? What good will it be to us to have glittering gold to adorn our bodies if there is no food and our stomachs will be eternally famished?" – *Mother Petra*

Connections between the health of our bodies and health of the land are critical for all women incubating new life everywhere, but especially for those who are taught and given the privilege to nurture ancestral bonds to a storied and sacred place. As a child, after packing our balikbayan boxes and saying our evening prayers, Lola Mary would share stories of evacuation on the day the Japanese bombed Baguio[2], her long

---

[2] On December 7, 1941, many often take time to remember the bombing of Pearl Harbor. It is also important to note, that ten hours after the attack in Honolulu, the mountain city of Baguio was also bombed on December 8, 1941 and later taken and occupied for another four years. Almost simultaneously, after the Japanese attack on Pearl Harbor, the Army confiscated 6,600 acres in and around Makua valley on Oahu to train troops for World War II, evicting ranchers and families who lived there. It still occupies nearly 4,200 acres today. Makua, unfortunately, till this day has never been given back.

walk home on Kennon Road, and how she carried my father on her back and held my auntie by the hand as they sought refuge during the World War II brown-outs on the mountain side. She never ceased talking about the beauty of the rice terraces and her people through songs and stories. It was often her homesickness and my reading letters from home that prompted me to keep alive, some connection to the Cordillera, in my adulthood.

Later in my early twenties, I remember learning more about the Cordillera land struggles against extractive mining and the story of the Chico River Dam and the struggle from attending the annual summer East Coast Grand Canao. What impressed me most about the story, aside from the fact that it was performed by diasporic Igorot youth, was the bold collective action taken by the women and the villagers to defend their land. I was struck by how deeply people cared for a place and how it was the land that "owned" them, not the other way around. I was also struck that those of us in this generation, living in the U.S. struggled to keep the memory alive. We have been fortunate to learn and know our dances and play gangsa (gong). We have been fortunate to know that taste of tapuey and the feeling of being present at the sacrifice of a chicken or a pig. But some of us still have not known the feeling of feeding ourselves from camote, gabi, or gulay that we had grown with our own hands or feel the sensation of Kanakaney ogayam on our tongues. Many of us do not know how to chant the land back to life. As I became a mother in Hawai'i, away from my own family, this became especially important, as I decided to stay on, birth, and raise Malaya on ka pae aina (land) where kanaka maoli face similar challenges and struggles.

I remember one of my last trips with my parents back home to the Philippines, of walking through the rice fields in both Tadian and in Cervantes and noticing the rows of gabi or taro planted right alongside the rice fields and a river. If I had been living anywhere else, I may have seen the taro, or kalo in Hawaiian, as simply another tuber variety. However, living in Hawai'i, I understand this plant as far more significant as canoe plant and I recognize it by its other name, haloa, an older sibling that joins us as relatives across the Pacific. In fact, according to anthropology professor Stephen Acabado, the idea that the taro could be the first staple crop before rice in the Cordillera is not new; taro is planted ceremonially, even in the coastal Ilocos.

If this true, a new set of questions must be asked: What do I owe this place that has connected me to me, a place that has served as my grounding to malama honua (care for Mother Earth)? What is my kuleana (responsibility)? What do I also owe to ka po'e kahiko to re-bridge our peoples? Malaya's umbilical cord and placenta remain in Hawai'i and thus, it is her pusod and piko that is buried here. She is planted here with others like her and in that vein, it is her legacy now to continue and her lessons to carry.

Malaya, Grace, and Paul Tuan Tran.

 *As an early literacy and parent educator in her community of Kalihi, Grace Alvaro Caligtan works to restore familial connections to places and stories from where one calls home. In this same vein, she roots herself in service to pregnant and birthing families and the ancestral wisdom that comes from being a witness at the portals of life. The honor of being at this rite of passage also inspires Grace to advocate for public policy that upholds the dignity, bodily autonomy, and self-knowing of all women. She is currently a Community Outreach Educator for Planned Parenthood of Great Northwest and Hawaiian Islands.*

Ten

SUMPA, USOG, AND OTHER
SPIRIT-WORLD HEALING PRACTICES

by Divina Telan Robillard

Thirty-one years. Half of my life and most of my marriage were spent taking care of my husband, Britt. First, on a part-time basis, then when his care became more complicated, I quit my job to be his fulltime caregiver. In late 1984, when Britt's primary physician tentatively diagnosed him to have Amyotrophic Lateral Sclerosis (ALS) or Lou Gehrig's disease, it felt like we were being handed a death sentence. The shock was so extreme that, for many years afterwards, Britt would lead both of us onto the trail of many neurologists, physician friends, tests, clinics, more tests in pursuit of a diagnosis that was more palatable, acceptable, non-disabling, non-fatal. In late 1984, we had been married barely a year and half.

As a new bride, I felt the repercussion of those shock waves in many ways and meanings other than those Britt personally experienced. What would a disabling disease mean for me, the wife? What about my career plans and dreams? How do I secure my financial life, especially if he passes early? Where/when will a "normal" life be available to Britt and me? Because of the centrality of having a family of my own, should I even think of conceiving, with a disabled dad for our children? If Britt were to die early, how would I cope with early widowhood, and our children, with being orphans? Should I even stay in this marriage, given that, married only a few days before my 29th birthday, my biological clock was ticking?

I was a new immigrant and a stranger to Hawai'i. I had

no friends of my own. I knew no one outside of Britt's brother and sister and their families on island, and two nurses whom I had befriended sitting for the NCLEX-RN licensure examination. Like me, they were newly arrived in the USA. These were a few of the questions that circled around my head, like a silent swarm of salivating vultures patiently anticipating their swooping attack.

In the early 1980s, not much was known about ALS and its treatment. In 1939, it struck the baseball legend NY Yankee Lou Gehrig. At the peak of his career, Gehrig gave up playing because of ALS. His name is now synonymous with that tongue-twister of a disease so that people could easily recall what ALS could do to anyone, even a baseball great like him. ALS was, and is, to this day, considered a rare and orphan disease. A "rare disease" is defined to affect less than 200,000 people at any one time. An "orphan disease" is one that "has not been 'adopted' by the pharmaceutical industry because it provides little financial incentive for the private sector to make and market new medications to treat or prevent it."

Back home in Manila, news of Britt's diagnosis rocked my family like no upheaval could. Britt and I were just too far away from my family who felt helpless, and unable to provide even the physical presence to show support. Phone calls between Manila and Hawai'i became more frequent and shadowed by shared grief, worry, and more questions, none of which had an answer.

Since 1869 when it was first described, ALS has been without known cause and cure. This dumbfounded my mother who then offered a supernatural explanation for Britt's illness. Perhaps, my husband's ex-wife put a sumpa (curse) on him? Britt's divorce was anything but friendly and was fraught with pain. Even though interactions between the exes were civil and few, they were palpably tense.

In consultation with her sisters and friends, my mother would search for opinions as to origin and cure of the disease, thereby exposing my haole (Caucasian) husband to various interpretations of disease causation as well as treatments. Initially, I pooh-poohed my mother's attempt at a spirit-world theory of the origin (and therefore, a cure) of Britt's illness. Britt's ex-wife was second generation Chinese-American and, by being so removed from the motherland, I doubted that she would be inclined to use this kind of retribution.

"Kahit na," my very traditional Mom said, "Intsik ang kaniyang pamilya. Malay natin? Hindi lang natin alam kung ano ang kanilang paniniwala sa larangan ng espirito?" ("Even so. Her family is Chinese. Who knows? We just don't know what their spirit-world beliefs are.")

And so it was that a number of traditional rituals and beliefs were practiced. Because of the urgency complicated by distance, my Mom asked that an unwashed shirt of Britt's—one that still bears his sweat and body oils—be sent home. The shirt traveled with a family friend to my home province of Cagayan where the help of a minangngilu (practitioner of hilot or healing massage) was solicited to ask for mercy from the spirit-world, reverse the sumpa, and cure Britt's illness. Furthermore, my cultural interpreter-mother suggested that, perhaps, Britt's purchase of a single bulol (rice god) from one of our earlier travels to Baguio has angered its partner. Rice gods were supposed to come in pairs. To my mother, it didn't matter that the bulol we purchased was already without its partner in the shop when we bought it in the first place. Being party to the further separation of the bulol from its partner was enough to cause a disturbance in the spirit-world, leading to disequilibrium and anger; thus, the illness. Britt thought this explanation made perfect sense so I sent home the bulol, asking my family to have the wooden statue returned to the shop from where it was bought.

Britt was already developing signs of ALS early in 1984, although they started as seemingly innocuous muscle tics. His right pointer finger would occasionally involuntarily "jump,"

83

Bulol can be viewed at the Honolulu Museum of Art Philippine Collection.

even while his hand was at rest. This twitch would be accompanied by muscle tremors on the back of the hand. Initially, his internist friend corroborated our dismissal of these as signs of stress. After all, Britt was working very hard writing grants to maintain his temporary Associate Professor status at the University of Hawai'i School of Medicine (UHSM) Department of Psychiatry. He had also been in at least three life changes in the past two years: Divorce; remarriage; and the death of his mother. But life changes notwithstanding, life had to move on. So, during the time that he was experiencing these early symptoms, he applied for a Fulbright Research Grant to study community-based health care delivery systems in the Philippines.

Community-based health systems and their component parts were where our individual research and teaching experiences merged beautifully. My work in teaching primary health workers in rural areas was totally in sync with his own foray into training mental health workers in Micronesia. This was the common interest that led us both to converge in Pohnpei in 1982. I was then a short-term consultant for the World Health Organization Western Pacific Regional Office in Manila while on leave as faculty at the University of the Philippines College of Nursing. He was a behavioral scientist at the UHSM Psychiatry department. As fate would have it, we were to marry late that year after a whirlwind bi-continental courtship, most of which was conducted via snail mail.

Getting the prestigious and generous award definitely brought Britt the pride and excitement he deserved. But these emotions were toned down by the grim presence of increasingly crippling muscle wasting. The Fulbright grant was to take us to Manila as the base for his research into community-based health programs (CBHP's) for eight months. When we arrived in Manila in January 1985 his right hand was already visibly atrophied and weakness in that arm was affecting his ability to write by hand and hold onto anything heavier than a hardcover book.

Upon our arrival at home, my mother immediately performed one of the rituals she and my paternal grandmother before her used to do, when, as children, we would experience unexplained disorders. It is based on the Filipino belief called usog or bati. This ritual had always fascinated me and so when I became an older adult, I chose to learn it from my mother, in anticipation of future motherhood. Among the many spirit-world beliefs to which my family subscribed, it was usog that was most compatible with my other belief systems.

Researchers tell us that, in many clusters of our diverse country, there is a belief in a soul that is capable of leaving the body temporarily. If this absence is prolonged, the owner may get sick or die. This wandering tendency of the soul implies that the soul is capable of leaving on its own, especially when "frightened," for example, by loud noises, attacking animals, and strangers. When a person's (especially a child's) soul leaves, he/she is said to be na-usog. A theory similar to usog is bati, wherein the sight of or expressed admiration by strangers, who are deemed to have a much stronger spirit power than the na-bati, overwhelms the person's soul, thus, making it flee.

In my home province of Cagayan, Ybanags like our family have a similar belief in usog. In our case, we call the predicament, nawawan y-c cararrua (soul loss). My mother taught me how to coax the lost soul back to its owner by the performance of a ritual that is part-indigenous and part-Christian. She would choose to perform this ritual towards dusk. Chanting the incantation in the gathering darkness finds rhythm with the cricket chirps and sounds of chicken roosting in the night. In the rural Tuguegarao of my youth, she would gather five to six seeds of palay (unhusked rice), which she would proceed to de-husk in order to get the whole grain, including the germ. When we moved to the city in later years, processed rice in place of palay, became acceptable for this rite.

With flickering light dramatically emanating from an old kerosene lamp, she would hold the grains of rice in the palm of her hand and chant the following three times in the presence of the sick child: "Anno-c atta, arriyammu panawan si (name of person), awan tu kagayam." ("Anno-c atta, don't leave (name of person); he/she won't have a play/soulmate.") She would then pray the Our Father three times, after which she'd make the sign of the cross three times over a small bowl of water before dropping the grains into the bowl. This part is chicken-skin time, when, silently and with purpose, tipping the bowl this way and that, she would peer in to see which grains (and how many) had a bubble or two on top.

We would crowd closer to her as seconds ticked away. Then, with eyes transfixed on the tiny, iridescent globule of air sitting atop a grain, her face would crease into a triumphant smile and say, "Hayun. Hayun na siya." ("There. There it is.") With pursed lips and tip of the head, she'd point its location out to us. This was the sought for sign that the person has been na-usog. To complete the ritual, she scoops the rice and captures the bubble with a cotton ball, squeezes out the water that gets retrieved with the rice grains, and deposits them into a gauze pad or small piece of cloth. Afterwards, the na-usog is made to sip a little water from the bowl. The cloth or pad is rolled around the grains and both ends secured with a tie. Once secured, the piece of cloth is attached to the na-usog's clothing with a safety pin. It is kept pinned on until the person recovers from the ailment.

Would that a cure for ALS be this easily attainable! Alas, Britt's illness would continue unabated, eventually taking away the ability to move his limbs and confining him to a wheelchair. After a mismanaged bout of pneumonia that brought him to near respiratory failure, our yearning for a cure would be replaced by a kind of reluctant acceptance. However, it would surface every so often, invariably stimulated by someone offering another attempt to summon the spirit-world or learning of a newly found miracle herb or new-fangled technology. Although we were always hopeful, there came a time when we would merely smile at these suggestions. Life longed to be lived.

Is there a place, then, for these traditional beliefs in the diaspora? Since the dawn of time, humans have found it useful to believe in a parallel universe populated by the Unknown, whose mood and behavior impact human lives. Therefore, whenever health and wellbeing are at risk, theories related to their achievement and maintenance will be summoned. Belief in shamans, the abundance of god mythologies, and present-day ideas of a monotheistic God are ample evidences of our predisposition towards seeking other-world explanations of phenomena that affect our lives.

In the context of Britt's illness, traditional healing offered meaning when there was none. It gave solace, comfort, and support when such were meager and intermittent. It had a role to play in our life at that stage of the illness. When Britt was first diagnosed in late 1984, he was already staring at death within two to five years. What could be more devastating than that? Death at 45 would mean so many things: No more late night walks on Kailua beach; no more spontaneous trips to McCully Chopsuey for thick, wide noodles buried in crunchy bean sprouts and black bean sauce; no more witnessing births, attending weddings, or participating in the joy of having grand children. Face to face with one's mortality, one grabs at straws, no matter how fragile.

As it turned out, Britt did not die at 45, or at 47. In fact, he lived to be 72, thirty-one more years of productive life, both personal and academic, since the diagnosis. We got pregnant and had a son, Thomas, who at the time of Britt's death was 28 years of age, had completed college, was in a serious relationship, and thinking of a second career. Britt had that one and only health setback, mentioned earlier. Following that and despite his doctor's grim predictions, Britt went back to work after three months in the hospital. He would never be hospitalized again.

Of course, that pragmatic decision to keep him at home

despite his need for skilled nursing care meant that I would be at work with him as his fulltime caregiver, now sans a future in academic nursing. But go back to work, he did: Teaching graduate courses with colleagues; writing a book on his illness and editing another; and getting promoted to full professor. Who could tell if any one of these achievements, both longevity and productivity, was due to the mystery-shrouded rituals of a minangngilu-c hovering over a sweaty aloha shirt, or the simple incantations of a mother, desperate to erase that which causes her children pain? Or for that matter, the many candles lit in front of altars, jos sticks kindled in temples, and the many prayers murmured on bended knees by friends and family?

During the many years that Britt thrived despite ALS, new families living with ALS frequently turned to me for advice, particularly the use of alternative healing arts such as acupressure, acupuncture, herbs, and "faith healing." It always tore my heart to see families dipping into their shrinking purses to pay for alternative/complementary healing methods, majority of which are unproven and hence, cannot be reimbursed by our insurance system. And yet, I believe that there are forces out there beyond our limited understanding which help shape our destinies in this world. This belief would lead me to respond pragmatically, tempering my answer with caution by laying out the pros and cons of their use.

Undeniably, our culture is rich with a folklore filled with higante (giant), mangkukulam (sorceress), and other colorful spirits whose alleged activities intrude into our daily lives. Our traditions are there, some in their pristine state and others, evolving to be relevant (and acceptable) to the situations they are practiced. Reaching out to this treasure trove of the spirit-world enables us to participate in their continued relevance in our lives as we disperse to the further reaches of our planet. It unites us with our forebears and to the people we leave behind in the motherland, thus carrying along with us the very Filipino-ness that makes us distinct from others. And yet, because of the common source of our earthly lore—our human desire to be one with the other world—it truly allows us also, to be one with the real world.

 *Divina Telan Robillard, BSN, RN, MPH, has been a nurse educator since graduation from college in 1976. She is currently writing a book based on her 31 years of experience as her husband Britt's primary caregiver. She volunteers for efforts targeted to better care for ALS families and especially with a group seeking to establish an ALS House in Hawai'i.*

Eleven
THE FINAL PASSAGE
by Virgie Chattergy

Looking Back

My grandmother was in her late nineties when she passed away. She had 11 children but only four survived her. My family moved her from the little room in our house where she stayed for the last few years, and into a bedroom that I shared with my sister the morning they felt would be her last, because our room was slightly more spacious. She died in our room. I was ten years old.

I remember that day very well. The school I attended was holding a one-day retreat for its students in the elementary grades. We were all in church that morning and as soon as we were dismissed for the noon break, my cousin came running to me and my sister, urging us to go home as quickly as possible as our grandmother lay dying.

The church was located directly across the street from where we lived, so it was only a matter of minutes before we reached the house and were ushered into our room. I was surprised and confused because she wasn't there when we left that morning. My grandmother was lying in bed, her wrinkled tiny hands resting on her chest, clasping a rosary. Her eyes were closed and you would have to go close up to her face to see if she was still breathing. My sister and I were told to put our hands over hers and to say that we were there. In the stillness of the room, you could hear a pin drop. As we touched her hands that had already grown cold, two of her fingers quivered in response, then dropped and the weight of her whole tiny body

91

seemed to drop into the bed. Then, someone whispered that she was "gone." We were told that she waited for my sister and me to get there to say goodbye and that she was in that condition most of the morning. She didn't want to die without saying goodbye.

The memory of that morning has stayed with me because I didn't realize how much we meant to her. I was especially moved because I caused her so much grief. My sister, who was older only by a couple of years, was the ideal daughter and granddaughter and I was the rascal who had to be watched and disciplined all the time. My grandmother use to carry a horsewhip to make me do what she expected, be it finishing my meals or taking siesta on weekends. She never hit me with it, just threatened me. By the time I was in grade school, she had what we now know as macular degeneration, so she could only see dimly. I had fun evading her by calling out to her, then darting over to another place.

Once, she caught me in the bathroom where there was only one way in and one way out, so I was trapped when she appeared at the door. I screamed my lungs out and my sister saved me by guiding my grandmother to one side so I could slip out. That was the last time I tried to tease my lola. She told us ghost stories to put us to sleep because she believed that in fright, we would close our eyes and therefore, fall asleep sooner. I pretended and went along with her and strangely enough, I did fall asleep before she finished telling her stories of the agta and other mythical creatures. Just in case you are wondering, no, I didn't use that strategy with my own children. But I did grow up learning all about the "spirit world" of the early Filipinos before they were replaced by Christian images of saints.

My grandmother's children, their families and friends, grand children and great grand children were present at her bedside soon after she died. In the presence of a priest, the atmosphere was prayerful, emotions were subdued and voices were hushed. The torrent of tears and passionate crying would come later. For the next two days, the wake was in our living room. People in the neighborhood flowed in and out of the house, day and night. Evening prayers lasted nine consecutive evenings when snacks and drinks were served, including beer and tuba (fermented coconut) taken in moderation, out of respect.

In our culture, funerals, like baptisms and weddings are occasions for social interaction. There was much in the atmosphere that suggested a celebration although the mourning was sincere. Friends and relatives recalled and exchanged joyous and amusing anecdotes about my grandmother. Our room was cleaned up and we continued to sleep and use the room as we always had, without fear, anxiety or concern that someone had just died in that room. We accepted death as natural and inevitable. She was, after all, our grandmother who took care of us daily and we knew she loved us.

We respected her in life; we were to respect her memory in death—a caring, and supportive lola with unconditional love for the apo. This I wanted to believe with all my heart but I had a little difficulty during the wake. Her body was laid to rest in an open casket in the living room that was upstairs. I had to walk pass it, to go in and out of the bedroom and to go in and out of the house, which meant also going downstairs where the visitors gathered. They came upstairs to pay their respects, pray and go downstairs to socialize with other mourners.

As long as there was someone with me, I was perfectly at ease, but I remember one instance when I had to go upstairs by myself. Will she sit up when I pass by to show her disapproval over my disobedience? I can still picture in my mind's eye, those few seconds when I inched my way against the wall, never leaving my gaze from her coffin. I don't remember if I was daring her to appear or daring her NOT to appear. What I would have done if she did, I know not! The whole episode only took 20 seconds, but it seemed like two hours! Other than this, much of what happened regarding the services is blurry in my memory. I wish now that I had more time with my grandmother because I am now, myself, a grandmother. I think I would have behaved a whole lot better than I did, instead of being such a troublemaker.

Fast Forward

I experienced, for the first time and close up, some of the Philippine traditions surrounding the care of someone facing the end of life 42 years after my grandmother's death. This time, I was a front-line participant at my mother's final years and burial rites.

A long distance call from Cebu to Honolulu signaled the beginning of her end: "Your mother had a major stroke and is in intensive care in the hospital." My sister from Virginia immediately arranged to fly home. I had to wrap up the last two weeks of spring semester at the University of Hawai'i, so I was to follow. My older son came home for the summer from a mainland college, and together we flew home to the Philippines. He is my mother's first grandson.

That first year, my mother was paralyzed on the right side but rallied to better health. She was able to move around in a wheel chair and tried to speak haltingly or write down what she wanted to say. In the second year, she was slowly getting frustrated with her situation and grew more helpless. In the third year, she needed 24-hour care and was practically bedridden. My sister and I hired two nurses to care for her, one for the night and the other, for the day. A cousin helped for two hours in the morning between the shifts. My mother, at this point, had more bad days than good. Good days basically meant that she could use her left arm to gesture and utter two or three words at a time. All together, she lived for three years and nine months after her stroke.

Conflicts with my cousins who were helping care for her in my absence began to surface whenever I returned home for a visit. One stands out in my mind to this day. My mother woke

94

up from deep sleep and said that her mother was in the room. "Why," she wanted to know, "was her mother in the room?" My cousins quickly dismissed what she said as nonsense and some kind of hallucination. I ignored their comments and asked my mother where my grandmother was in the room. She pointed to one corner of the room and I turned to look in the direction of her feeble gesture. Of course I knew no one was there but continued to ask her what her mother was doing? She answered haltingly, "Looking, looking at me."

I said to her, "Your mother is watching over you and trying to tell you not to be afraid because she is waiting on the other side to welcome you."

My mother gave me a look that I thought was one of relief and she went back to sleep. My cousins, meantime, were appalled! Was I wishing her to die? I explained that my mother needs peace, not aggravation. I pointed out the result—my mother went back to sleep. When she was contradicted and scolded, she would show anger in her face, stare, groan and emit sounds in the most disturbing way to show her displeasure. I told them to go along with what she said and let her imagine or dream—whatever it took to calm her down.

At another time, she woke up, wide eyed and said, "I'm afraid."

I asked "Of what?"

She looked at me and said, "The room, ngit-ngit" (dark) and big world."

It just so happened that the day before, I visited the cemetery plot she talked about a year before her stroke. She had bought a small burial plot complete with a coffin-like structure so she wouldn't be buried in the ground. This is not unusual for Filipinos. The coffin would be slid into the structure, intact. There was a small niche at the end of it where, per her wishes, she asked a cousin's bones to be laid so she would have company. At the top was a small and colorful statue of the Sacred Heart. An arch across the width of it had newly planted bougainvillea vines. Low wrought-iron bars surrounded the entire plot. She hired one of the cemetery caretakers to maintain the place. I was hugely impressed. Did she have a premonition of things to come?

I bent over to be close to her. "The dark room is only a place to hold your body because you're going to leave it to go into a beautiful big world where God will be waiting with your mother, father, and all your friends who are already there. One day, I too will go with you into the dark room." She looked at me for a few seconds and fell asleep. By now, the cousins left me alone to deal with these outbursts.

Day of Transition and Rituals

My mother passed away on the day of Cebu's most celebrated fiesta—Sinulog, a feast honoring the Child Jesus. Unlike my grandmother who died at home, my mother died in the hospital. The month before she passed away, I spent three weeks with her. Following my cousins' advise, I told her I was returning to Hawai'i the day before I was to leave, and that my sister would come to replace me. I promised to return after I had organized my classes for the University in the coming semester. She couldn't talk but her facial expression spoke volumes. She looked puzzled, pained, displeased and sad. Her eyes kept following me around the room. Around 5:00 a.m. the next day, I received a frantic call: "Your mother was taken to the hospital. She didn't sleep all night and is delirious."

I got ready, loaded my luggage in the car so I could go straight to the airport from the hospital and rushed over to see her. The nurse was relieved to see me. My mom was staring at me, and with all the strength she could muster, chanted repeatedly, "Balik, balik, balik (come back, come back)."

The nurse knew the meaning of the word but could not make sense out of the mantra. I explained that my mother wanted me to come back to bury her. I know I shocked the nurse with my straightforward response. Filipinos, generally, are not noted for their bluntness. That's just the way I am—calling

96

a spade, a spade.

I assured my mother that, yes, I will be back for her. The chanting stopped. Before I left, a short meeting with the doctor was in order. He said that my mother's body had just about given up on her but her brain kept going. Her body was rejecting even electronic feeding, but her mind was very much alive. Should she have another stroke or grow weaker, did he have my permission, not to resuscitate? I gave him permission to make her comfortable as she had been sick for so long and had become skin and bones. I left and my sister arrived the next day. She stayed with my mother all day and most of the night. Everyone urged her to rest as my mother was in good hands. The one day that my sister left her bedside to attend mass on Sinulog day, she was asked to return to the hospital immediately. She half ran, half walked because there were no taxis available. The whole city was in a celebratory mood.

Meantime, that Saturday morning (Sunday in the Philippines), I spent most of the day prepping for my substitute. I was to leave at dawn to return home as I promised. By five that evening, I was shopping for fruits to bring back to my sister. I was leaving the grocery and walking to my car when something stopped me in my tracks, something that was not of my own will. I stood rooted to the ground and felt a sensation that will stay with me for the rest of my life. An energy that felt like electricity zigzagged through me from head to toe, so fast, so clear and so powerful. I whispered, "Goodbye, Mama. Rest in Peace."

Where the day started with rain and dark clouds, the evening was clear and the moon shone brightly. I found myself singing a hymn as I drove home. I barely turned off the engine when my husband came running out to the carport. He never does this. He excitedly said that Sauntri, my best friend in Cebu called.

"To say my mother died?"

"How did you know?" he asked in surprise.

97

"She visited me to say goodbye." And I explained what I thought happened. My husband, who is East Indian, had no difficulty believing what I said. Indians also believe in spirits and life after death.

As soon as I arrived in Cebu, I was told not to drop a tear on the coffin. This would be one of several "rules" I had to honor but for which there were no explanations. Another was to leave a nail in the coffin. My cousins had forgotten to do this, so they opened the coffin to slip a nail in. My sister took the opportunity to move a strand of hair away from my mother's face. She was severely reprimanded. She was told that it disturbs the dead.

There were three nights for the wake. My sister slept on my mom's bed for two of those nights and I was assigned one night. Kids of various ages slept on the floor around the bed. They were all anxious to talk to me and tell stories. So, between the chatting late into the night, and the mahjong players shifting the tiles as they played until dawn, I considered the evening not a night of rest, but part of the ritual surrounding a wake at home.

The nine-day novena commenced. I was gratified to see some former teachers, nuns and friends attend. A woman whose job apparently was to lead nine-day novenas for the dead was hired and she chanted and rattled off in a sing-song manner a string of prayers that combined Visayan, Latin and Spanish all in one. We only had to respond with "Sancta Maria, Madre de Dios" and "Amen." They were long prayers. Light and simple meals were served. The big dinner for the neighborhood was reserved for the last night of the novena.

Prior to inurnment, the casket had to be taken to the church for mass. Another rule was for my sister and me to walk in front of the coffin, carried by relatives. We were not to look back until after we entered the church. Something about not making the dead reluctant to leave if one looks back, I was told. We expected one priest to officiate at mass but another one showed up who was close to the family. The con-celebration and high mass with a choir singing my mother's favorite hymns clinched the formal religious rite.

A procession to the cemetery followed mass services. A cousin who was a policeman, organized six of his friends to lead the way. In their uniforms and on their motorcycles, they formed an upside-down V formation. The car carrying the bier was within the formation and the mourners walked behind, side by side, six to eight in a row. The car moved ever so slowly, streaming hymns from its loudspeaker like, "Nearer my God to Thee." My mother would have approved.

Since we occupied the main road, cars and jeepneys squeezed by the sides or stopped to let us pass. I was surprised when the drivers beeped the horns in sympathy (no one yelled annoyance over their slight delay) and threw pesos or coins our way. Strangers would stop and make the sign of the cross as we passed and some would also donate money. Two young kids came prepared. They carried jars and walked at the ends of the line, one on each row in front. They knew what to do. They accepted or ran after monies thrown our way. I worried over their safety as they were close to the moving cars. We arrived safely after a slow and comfortable 40-minute walk where we recited the rosary along the way. My mother was properly interred. Some snacks were provided at the cemetery.

We were not allowed to visit the graveside until after three days after inurnment; never heard of this rule before in my life. Tempted as my sister and I were to break that rule, we were too intimidated and stayed away for the required three days before visiting again. When we returned, we noticed that the cement in front of the burial door through which the coffin was interred had hardened. Finally, I realized that I was never going to see my mother alive again. There is something so final about death that makes me glad that I was raised to believe that the spirit lives on.

Lessons learned

My first thoughts are about my mother's foresight, thoughtfulness, and preparedness to handle her own end-of-life challenges. She relieved my sister and me of any anxiety about what to do. She gave clear instructions to our cousin about her wishes, such as the wake at home, no embalming, burial on the third day (she was sure we would be there for her in time), and she had prepared her own place of rest, all taken cared of monetarily.

Am I ready to do the same for my children? Not quite. It is an enormous responsibility for which I have less courage than my mother had. Perhaps, I, too, will have some premonition that will motivate me to be prepared before my time comes.

Compared to my mother's celebration of life at the end, how like or unlike will mine be? For starters, no wake at home! Nine-day novena? I doubt it. As an aside, I read somewhere that the nine-day novena resonated with a pre-Spanish tradition brought over by the Malays. The Malay people, who were one of the two major groups who migrated to the Philippines (the other being Indonesians) long before our contact with the West, believed that the dead did not leave the earth but stayed around for nine days after his/her death—hence the vigil to accompany the Spirit while still with family and friends, though no longer with the body.

I think the rituals and customs I experienced at my mother's funeral reflected practices within a specific region, and perhaps, even more specific to a given community. This is easy to understand when we realize that the Philippines is so diverse, with mountain ranges that separate islands east from the west and north from the south. Furthermore, being an archipelago, the different islands are strung across miles of ocean. Understandably, rituals surrounding major life transitions like births, marriages, and deaths are as varied as are the languages spoken in the different regions, in spite of similarities across.

I haven't participated in funerary services in Cebu since I left in the 1960s. I suspect that there are no major differences in terms of how the church in different areas of the world offers prayers for the departed. However, there are customs particular to Filipinos that find their way into these ceremonies. A good example is church weddings. Essentially, this ceremony is the same from the perspective of the church, but Filipinos vary in how this ritual is conducted from one province to the next. So, too, are the ways used to mark other transitions. In addition to indigenous practices, these rituals may reflect other cultures that have impacted Filipinos from pre-Spanish times, e.g. influences of the Muslims, the East Indians, and the Chinese with whom we have interacted long before the West came.

Not having these rituals is not a problem with me. The challenge I face is in determining what I believe are essential from past practices, and therefore, should be maintained vis-à-vis what is practical, given my present day reality. I don't know the answer today. However, I do know that unlike my grandmother and mother, cremation is the practical way for me to exit. After all, "from dust....unto dust."

Virgie Chattergy is professor emeritus from University of Hawai'i Manoa. She received her postgraduate degrees from UCLA. Born, raised, and educated in Cebu, Philippines, she received a degree in elementary education from St. Theresa's College. She pioneered the inclusion of language sensitivity and cultural diversity in education programs at UH Manoa at a time when the idea was new. Her involvement led to a variety of awards including NEA's "Leadership in Asia/Pacific Island Education."

Twelve

END-OF-LIFE CUSTOMS OF FILIPINOS IN HAWAI'I
by Bernice Ramos Clark

It was the fall of 1957 and I was three-and-a-half years old. Bright red blood spread quickly on white tissues, missing the wastebasket. I saw my mother and Apo Delfina attending to Apo Ok who was on the bed, hemorrhaging out of control. They made no attempt to get me out of the room. Everything was happening so quickly. An ambulance was called and he was taken to the hospital.

The next time I saw him was in a coffin, in the sala of their plantation home. People were arriving to pay their respect at his wake. Someone carried me up for one last look and let me make a sign of the cross on his body. I don't recall resisting nor being afraid.

Meanwhile, Uncle Filomeno was casting a makeshift cross out of cement. Before it set completely, he wrote the name and dates with a nail. The inscription was later finished with black paint.

The service was at St. Roch Catholic Church in Kahuku. It was customary to take a group picture with the coffin set in the middle.

Apo Ok was buried at a Christian cemetery near the edge of the golf course. I remember my dad packed his anteojos (glasses) in its case, and his violin in the coffin, along with other plantation-related items he might need in the next life. Apo Ok was only 51 years old.

In years that followed, I remembered the special altars set aside: Religious statuettes; offerings of food; boiled eggs; tabako or betel nut; kankanen and drink. Our meals would not begin without properly honoring the departed.

Years later, the cemetery had fallen into disrepair and his remains were reinterred at Hawaiian Memorial Park in Kaneohe to be with family and Vintar town mates who purchased plots/plans around the same time. In retrospect, the family should have kept Apo Ok's violin. It had, by then, disintegrated.

At other funerals during my childhood, I remember frequent and seemingly spontaneous wailing at the coffin, both at the masses and wakes. Young ones wore white with black ribbons decorating the arms or chest area. The widows wore black for the entire year. Novenas were said at the homes.

At a special gathering in the home, women prepared an herbal, diluted shampoo, used to wash the neck area of close relatives. It was a type of purification ritual meant to ward off harmful spirits. Once, my then pregnant sister was told by the ladies to stay in the car and not approach the graves at a cemetery. It was bad luck, they said.

In Hawai'i, it is not uncommon to continue or modify past practices from the Ilokos as long as it helps to strengthen bonds among town mates and within families, and to acknowledge the contributions of those ancestors who laid the foundations for the life we enjoy today. Because children have actively witnessed and participated in funeral rituals among different generations, a greater reverence and respect for tradition will continue. Children have less fear of the unknown.

Bernice Clark was born at the Kahuku Sugar Plantation, the fourth of 13 children of sakada Angel and Marcelina Ramos. She has a BA in Philippine Studies and an MSW in Social Development from the University of Hawai'i at Manoa. She is a Department of Education substitute teacher and lives in Honolulu with husband Michael, and daughters Marcella and Maya.

Thirteen
DAYAW
by Josephine Dicsen Pablo

Dayaw. Respect in Ilokano. It means to be considered worthy of high regard. To show respect is second nature to children in the Philippines. Children are expected to address elders using the proper honorific terms: Apong, Lola or Lolo (grandparents); Tatang/Nanang (parents); Manang/Manong (older siblings); Ninong/Ninang (godparents); Uncle/Auntie and so forth.

I am the oldest in a family of four and so was used to being addressed as "Manang." As a teacher in high school and college, I was "Miss" or "Ma'am," "Madam." To my nephews or nieces, I was "Auntie."

During a recent visit to the Philippines (2016), I became more aware of the expressions of respect, verbal or non-verbal. I realized how much I have missed being addressed respectfully, after having lived in Hawai'i for 48 years—more years than I have spent in my country of birth. Even attendants at Philippine Air Lines addressed me with "po," another expression of respect whenever I asked a question or when I was given information. What a great feeling!

At home in Baguio, nephews, nieces and their children ranging in age from five to 20, lined up to do mano, the traditional practice of putting the back palm or hand of the parent or older person on the child's forehead or kissing the hand/ring of a bishop as a sign of respect. After attending Sunday mass at a local church in Laoac, Manaoag (my husband's birthplace), I noted that most of the parishioners, including the elderly, lined up not to shake hands with the priest, but to mano. In this case, the bishop or priest placed his palm on the head of the person to be blessed, making a sign of the cross on the person's forehead. I was eager to be part of the line. Age didn't matter. Young or old, you showed respect using these gestures.

People around will remind you, lest you forget.

I remember vividly how we were taught to show respect for our teachers in a Catholic girls' high school that was administered by the Augustinian nuns (at that time, mostly from Belgium).

Our lay teachers were graduates of their colleges and universities in Manila and neighboring provinces in the Ilocos and were committed to remain single to teach. As soon as we entered the classroom in a single file, we went to the right side of our desks, greeted the teacher, "Good morning, Sister or Reverend Mother or Miss_____," and curtsied (similar to greeting a royalty or VIP in Western Europe). Other rules of good behavior and respect included sitting up straight with hands clasped together on the desk, eyes on the teacher, listening with full attention and raising hands to answer or ask a question. For one thing, we developed good posture and self-discipline. We greeted visitors by standing together, addressing them properly. When I was a teacher in St. Louis University in Baguio, my students showed respect in different ways: By not answering back when reprimanded for being noisy, talking to a seatmate while the teacher was talking, gazing outside the window day dreaming instead of paying attention, or misbehaving as can be expected of teen boys, ages 12 to 13. I was only 21 years old, the youngest of three ladies among a faculty of men and priests. I tried to look mature, unsmiling and strict to command their respect. Respect was a cornerstone of establishing good discipline in the classroom.

Agmanoak—may I have your blessing—is the greeting used in this Laoac, Pangasinan church by niece Eileen while performing the mano with parish priest, Fr. Estephen Mark Espinosa.

In Hawai'i, my first teaching experience was at a Catholic school in Honolulu. I thought it would be an easy transition since I had experience as a student and teacher in Catholic schools. Not the same! The students, administrators (sisters from a religious order different from the one I knew) and the school culture were different. The school was co-ed and was

106

comprised of students in grades seven and eight. This age group is equivalent to the first year high school boys I taught in the Philippines.

What a culture shock! The students, especially the boys, were downright disrespectful: Ill mannered, noisy, unruly, prone to answering back, couldn't sit still nor pay attention when the teacher was talking. Was this not a Catholic school? Were the classroom rules for good student behavior so different? I started to lose my confidence as a teacher. Because of this, I only stayed two weeks. By then, I was a mother with a two-month-old son who had to be taken to a baby sitter so I could fulfill my profession. Additionally, I was trying to adjust to a new environment and different lifestyle. If the students had been respectful and disciplined, I would have stayed to prove that I can be both a good teacher and wife and mother.

After that short teaching experience, in 1975, I was hired as one of the first bilingual educational assistants (EAs) for the first demonstration project under ESEA Title VII. I was fortunate to be assigned to a public school in Kalihi. The first grade class was selected as a "demonstration class" because 80 percent were Filipinos. Of the 80 percent, half were newly arrived immigrants and were assessed as non-English or limited English speakers. In the first months working as an EA, I thought the regular teacher was too strict with the immigrant students. I could feel the hurt and shame in their eyes when they were punished or scolded for something I considered were minor infractions. The classroom rules, although not in writing, were constantly verbalized. As a result, the students were respectful, well behaved, and well disciplined. I then realized the importance of verbalizing and posting classroom rules, and noted that respect, though a universal value, is expressed in different ways. Cultures may share the same value but its expression varies. What is respectful in one culture is considered disrespectful or meaningless in another.

In 1980, I became an educational specialist for Bilingual/

Multicultural Education at the Hawai'i State Department of Education. I visited several schools statewide for more than 20 years, observing how regular and foreign-trained teachers practice classroom management. Several school administrators had expressed concern regarding the possible lack of classroom management skills of foreign-trained teachers working with the local students. There was no need to be concerned when it came to immigrant students. Filipino teachers were able to handle the ELL (English Language Learners) or students with limited English proficiency because they shared the same cultural values and expectations. Sadly, I think some ELLs know how to behave in school when they first arrive but change after they have become assimilated to the American or Western style of classroom behavior.

But foreign-trained teachers didn't seem comfortable teaching local students because, in their observation, these students "lacked discipline, were disrespectful, impolite, etc." I got to know some teachers who preferred to teach in private schools in spite of lesser pay compared to the pay in the public schools. As one Asian teacher who shared at the national Teacher of the Year award said, "It was easier to be the best teacher in my country (Thailand) than to be the best teacher in America because of the respect the students showed teachers." I agree because in the Philippines, as I remember my school days, the same is true. Teachers are held in high esteem and revered. This is especially true in relation to priests and nuns.

In the late 1980s, when there was a need for bilingual teachers in Ilokano, Samoan, Korean, Tagalog, and Micronesian languages, bilingual teachers proved that they had effective classroom management skills after some training in this area. Classroom Management was a required course for professional certification. I took it upon myself to develop courses for the UH Outreach College to prepare and train teachers in classroom management integrating multicultural education and character education. Respect as a universal value was included in the Character Education Program and was recommended by the Board of Education in the late 1990s. The goal was to improve discipline in the public school classrooms.

There is clearly a cultural difference in classroom management styles between the teachers' home country and what it is here in the U.S.A. Case in point is a story shared by educators Michael and Shiela Forman. Sheila, a Filipina, expected her children to "look down" when being reprimanded as a sign of respect for authority while Michael, a Caucasian or haole expected his children to look him "straight in the eye" for the same reason. In the classroom, local or regular classroom teachers, expect the "Michael treatment" from the immigrant or ELL students, while bilingual or foreign-trained teachers, expect the "Sheila treatment" from the local students. Some regular classroom teachers in the Classroom Management classes that I taught shared with me that they found newly arrived Filipino students to be very respectful. However, some teachers did not know what to do when they asked the students to "look them straight in the eye" and "they looked down at their toes." Other teachers shared that it took some time for the ELL students to stop addressing them as "Ma'am" (pronounced "mom").

A "silent stare from the teacher" works well in the Philippine setting. It does not work here. Using non-verbal means as a style of managing behavior is usually effective with our ELL students but not with local students. To get the respect of local students, teachers have to verbalize and include their expectations in the classroom rules.

There was much to learn about respect as manifested in one's culture. I told the teachers that I have former students in the Philippines teaching in the ELLs Program who still call me "Madam," "Ma'am" or "Mrs. Pablo." They also still offer to carry my bag, umbrella, baggage, and other stuff when I visit their schools on the neighbor islands. Their attention reminds me of the "good old days" when students would run to meet me so they could help with my load of books and classroom materials.

After retiring from the DOE in 2000, I was asked to be a catechist, a teacher in religious education for our parish. Initially, I refused because I was retired and had other plans. However, the director of Religious Education and my friends were persistent. Apparently, the current staff had difficulty with discipline in the class and the children were not learning. Some had already dropped out. It was just September, only the second month since classes started.

The teacher in me felt some kind of remorse for not helping. I decided to volunteer on a temporary basis, asking to co-lead the class. The class of 12 students was sixth to eighth grade and co-ed. I reminded myself that this is volunteer work, a ministry. No monetary reward, so it would be easy to get out any time, help the current staff, then leave. Well, so much for "temporary." I am now on my ninth year as a Religious Education teacher. I believe that teaching respect for authority and others had an effect on my long tenure. One of my students told her mother, a fellow catechist, that "Mrs. Pablo is tough and makes the best lumpia roll." I took that as a compliment.

One of the classroom rules I posted and discussed in the first month was respect one another. I also asked, "How do you express that?" The students came up with their own ideas of showing respect such as: Listen when the teacher is talking; address the teacher properly (I told them to address me as "Mrs. Pablo," my co-teachers as "Miss _____"); pay attention and raise your hand if you want to speak/ask question; ask permission to stand or when you wish to leave the room. So, if you want to summarize these rules of good behavior in one word, the word is RESPECT.

Other Filipino values related to respect are: Respecting life, respecting the dead, and respecting other people's beliefs and opinions (as long as they do not impose them on you). My younger sister, now a widow, shared with me that she emphasized with her six children "respect for their father" in spite of years of domestic abuse due to his being an alcoholic. After all, their father gave them life, cared and provided for them in a manner he thought was best under the circumstances. The value of utang na loob (Tagalog for gratitude) is closely related to the value of showing respect to parents.

One final word on respect has to do with marriage. Respect for each other is a foundation in this union of two people. In marriage, big or small problems can be solved by showing mutual respect. Mutual respect means recognizing the dignity of the other person as a child of the Creator. "God created us in His image and likeness; male and female He created us." (Genesis)

So what specific aspects do I want to pass on to my children, grand children, and generations of Filipinos? I made sure that my two children understood respect for authority, the elderly, and rules and the moral law at home, in school, and in the community. The honorific terms for father, mother, grandma, grandpa, auntie, uncle, teacher, reverend father or sister should be used appropriately and respectfully. In our home, the terms Uncle or Auntie are used not only for blood relations but for older friends and neighbors. The mano was to be practiced with the elderly (especially relatives from the Philippines); our children practiced the mano when they were in grade school, especially after Sunday mass. This gesture was eventually replaced by a hug or kiss on the forehead, as they grew older.

One other gesture that I cherish is when young people hold the hand of elderly people in order to guide them as they walk, cross the street, or go up and down a staircase; opening the door or giving up a seat in a bus; and allowing the elderly to go first in any line.

Is this asking too much? All I want is RESPECT!!!

Josephine Dicsen Pablo, M.A. (Science Education), M.Ed. (Curriculum & Instruction with emphasis in Bilingual/ Multicultural Education). A resident of Mililani, Hawai'i, Joey is originally from Baguio City, Philippines and was an instructor at Saint Louis University before coming to Hawai'i in 1968. She worked as an educational specialist for Bilingual Education/SEA and technical assistance coordinator at the Office of Instructional Services of the Hawai'i State Department of Education (DOE). A few years after retirement, she served as educational consultant for the DOE's Program for English Language Learners, and part-time instructor for the Outreach College, College of Education, University of Hawai'i at Manoa.

FINDING OUR WAY

Sampaguita (jasmine), national flower of the Philippines.

Fourteen
BAHALA NA
by Cecile Joaquin Yasay

A young woman in her twenties, holding back the tears, accompanied by two boys aged four and six, was about to board a plane departing from Manila to California.

I was her—as I ventured out of my comfort zone, knowing that I had deeply hurt the only man who gave me unconditional love, my father. This was the beginning of my new life, discovering the new "me."

My Childhood

My childhood was idyllic, sheltered from the reality of hardships that other families face. My parents spoiled all nine of us with life's comforts: a huge home with a pool; travels abroad; education from exclusive schools. But this was tempered by discipline and demonstrated Christian values.

My father took an assignment at the Philippine National Bank and the Philippine Mission to the United Nations and relocated his whole family to New York. I was a sophomore in high school. We may have moved to another country, but life in the Joaquin household remained the same. My parents continued to raise us the Filipino way, constantly reminding us not to adopt American values of individualism. We were told to respect our elders, to speak politely, and never to answer back.

Later, as a freshman at Marymount Manhattan College, my father would pick me up every Friday night and bring me back to school on Monday morning, cutting my time to socialize without supervision. Whenever I was given a "liberty"

114

pass to attend a party, I had to be home by the stroke of midnight, like Cinderella.

My Marriage

But how did I find myself leaving home at 25 with two small kids? I left my husband because of his abusive behavior and his immature ways. Like me, he was raised in a similar and protective environment.

For starters, we got married at an early age. At 18, I was in my teens. At 20, he was barely over his teen years. He was my first serious relationship. Our families were very close (our fathers were best friends from school), so I thought I was doing the right thing. I was proven wrong early on. Butch and I were far from ready to deal with the demands and expectations of a union like marriage that requires a mature attitude and response to problems. This situation was exacerbated by his dependence and closeness to his mom and I to my dad. We were not able to develop a strong bond that could have helped sustain our marriage. Why? Because when faced with a problem, we ran to our parents and they "solved" our problems.

We had major problems. For example, when I decided to go back to school to finish college, he denied me the use of the family car. So my dad bought me a car. We argued and fought about his late nights out, drinking or playing cards with friends. Every time that happened, the children and I would go back "home" to Mom and Dad. Butch would pick us up, apologize, and promise to change his behavior. Sadly, the change was short-lived and he would go back to his old ways. My mother-in-law, whom I highly respect, advised me to be patient and accept my role as a self-sacrificing wife. I regarded her views as too traditional, typical of her generation. It just was not me.

I returned to school to enroll in a master's degree in industrial psychology and to start a career in personnel management. The gap and resentment between us grew and the fights became more frequent. "Why are you building a career when there is enough money to sustain our lifestyle without working?" Butch questioned. He could not understand my desire for self-fulfillment and self-sufficiency. After all, we were given a completely furnished home on our wedding day. Monthly, we received ample financial support from our parents. Unlike most newlyweds, we did not have to rely on each other, never experiencing any "lean years." Some couples would consider this a blessing. For us, it hampered our growth as a couple.

We were blessed with two children, each with well-trained and capable nannies, so even parenting responsibilities were taken out of our hands. Our comfortable home life prevented us from developing our role as responsible parents.

For Filipinos, family problems are private. So every time I got physically beaten up because of my nagging, the doctors would arrive in an ambulance to treat me at home. This was possible because the family owned the hospital. Why couldn't I be more like other Filipino wives who suffered in silence, even when their husbands are out late every night?

Finally, I decided not to go back to our conjugal home. I moved with the children to my parents' home to avoid the fights. My parents' home was always open as a place of refuge. However, we continued to try and save our marriage. We came up with a plan. We would go to the United States to study and work on building our relationship away from our families. Unfortunately, when his mother opposed it, he accepted her position without an argument.

That was the turning point. I knew then I had to move away with the children. My older son, Nino, had started school grudgingly because he said that "only mommies go to school and work. Daddies just play golf and poker with friends." Obviously, it was not the direction I wanted my sons to follow. It was time for me to take responsibility for the proper upbringing of my children.

On My Own

Filipino parents never think of their children as old enough to be completely on their own and separated from them. So when I left, I was going against a deep-seated tradition. I love my parents, but I wanted to break the "curse", for the sake of my sons. I wanted to experience the value of hard work, of being appreciated for the work I do, not because of who my family was, but because I was deserving of recognition. I wanted to set an example for my children.

So the trip was planned without my parents' knowledge. I knew it would break their heart. It could even cause the break-up of our two families. I was ready to face the consequences, for the sake of my children.

After purchasing our plane tickets, I was left with $5,000—an inadequate sum knowing it will have to last until I find a job. I planned to apply at the United Nations, encouraged that my Dad's close friend, Mr. Rafael Salas, was the Executive Director of the United Nations Population Fund at that time.

On the day of our departure, I told my children we were going to Disneyland. I had made arrangements to stay with relatives in Los Angeles. That was such a treat for my two sons and the best way to begin our new life.

The change became immediately apparent. Without nannies, I took care of them myself. What an ordeal! Just giving them a bath was a handful! The first time I gave them a bath, we got soaking wet, with me fully clothed. The crying turned to uncontrolled laughter when we all found the humor in the situation. I was finally being a hands-on mother and enjoying it immensely.

A hotel close to the United Nations was our first home in New York. Against my better judgment, I left them at the hotel by themselves when I met Mr. Rafael Salas.

Mr. Salas promised me a job if I pass the pre-employment tests, which included typing. That scared me. I did not know how to type. As personnel officer in the Philippines, I had my own secretary to do my typing.

On my way home from the interview, I saw a "Now Renting" sign in front of a brand new luxury apartment a block away from the United Nations. I called my cousin Dr. Bobby Jimenez, who was living in Manhattan and he generously agreed to co-sign the lease with me. Within a week, we had moved into our new apartment. I was beginning to see that independence from my earthly father meant dependence on God, my heavenly Father, and He was taking care of us.

Challenges

We Filipinos are often criticized for our bahala na attitude, a lackadaisical reaction to new situations, presumably signifying irresponsibility. I started my new life with this attitude, but it was premised on taking the big leap with so much faith in God. Mine was "Bathala na"– (Bathala means God, so I leave it up to God, not to chance). And He manifested His presence and guidance throughout my journey into self-discovery.

Daily challenges in my new life included feeding my children since I knew nothing about cooking. Our apartment was brand new with a modern kitchen, but no furniture. Another challenge was stretching our funds, so I limited my purchase to essentials, such as a mattress with beddings, a pot and frying pan, a set of four plates, utensils and glasses, and a small black- and-white television. I bought cans of spam and learned to cook it in so many different ways: sliced very thin and fried, chopped with fried rice and eggs, as an omelet, etc. We ate this with rice and assorted boiled vegetables, bought frozen. Our suitcases served as the dining table.

It was January, with snow on the ground. I took the children shopping for winter clothes. Richie, my younger son, was always cold and shivering so I splurged on a down jacket for him, two sizes bigger so it could cover most of his body. I did not buy anything for myself until I got a job. When they asked to buy toys, I took them to the 69-cent shop and allowed them to choose one each. Even without money we had discovered happiness. A 69-cent toy given at the right time was more valuable than their expensive toys back home. Many times during our stay in New York, the children said that they were happiest when we were "poor."

I still had to face the biggest challenge—passing the typing test. Applicants are given three chances with each one scheduled a month apart. Pressure was building since we were only given a 6-month stay with our tourist visa. If I do not get the job at the United Nations which will convert our visas to a working one, we could not stay in the United States. Passing the typing test was the only hurdle.

Help from the Family

Upon landing in New York, I received a call from my dad's accountant. Though he had not spoken to me since I left, Dad nevertheless gave me access to his bank account. I did not accept his offer. A month later, my mother called to let me know that my sister Charo was enrolling at the Marymount College and they would be in New York. Upon arrival, my mother furnished our bare apartment, seemingly for Charo. Finally, we were sleeping in real beds again and eating from a dining table.

The Good News

After failing the typing test three times, I was getting discouraged. Every day I would go to mass with a single prayer, "God, help me pass the test." I even began to question Mr. Salas' promise of a job.

But when he gave me a fourth chance two days before my visa was going to expire, I knew I was going to make it. As I felt my fingers gliding through the keyboards, I was sure the Holy Spirit was taking the typing test with me. I passed! The next day, my visa was processed for conversion as a UN employee and I started working at my new entry level job, the level of a "go-fer." Nevertheless, the job was an answer to my prayer.

I experienced the same cliff-hanger situation many times. I believe that God tests your convictions and will give you what you are praying for only when you show some determination.

My New Life

The United Nations job provided me with a generous share of "humble pie." Where in the past, I had my own office and staff, I was now the lowest employee in the career ladder, a part of the typing pool. On my first day, I had to send out telegrams to UN offices all over the world, each with four carbon copies. With so many mistakes, I had to re-do each one several times. My trash can was full by the end of the day.

Though I felt sorry for myself, quitting was not an option. I was determined to make it on my own, for the sake of my children. The pain and daily challenges were necessary in developing my inner strength and character. Eventually, my efforts paid off, with promotions coming more quickly.

Eight years later, the same Cecile who joined the UN at the messenger level was now being re-hired by the United Nations Development Programme as conference officer, and given my own office. To get there, I took a chance of leaving the UN to work at the International Planned Parenthood Federation. If I had stayed on, it would have taken me more than 20 years to be an officer. Because of the excellent pay, benefits and job security, nobody resigns from the United Nations.

I took the gamble and it worked. My faith-filled life opened this opportunity which I took without flinching.

Eventually, several of my siblings moved to New York, as well as my parents who shuttled between Manila and New York. My father bought each of us homes in the same Long Island neighborhood. This time, I accepted his gift, knowing that I was not dependent on it. Besides, it afforded my children the chance to grow up with their cousins, aunts, uncles, and their grandparents.

I finally left the United Nations and New York for good after 15 years when I was given a second chance at marriage to Perfecto, the son of a Protestant pastor and a school teacher. With maturity, I now understood that the husband was the head of the household. I had no business entering into another marriage if I could not accept it.

We started off on the right foot, because he took his leadership role seriously, even accepting the care of my two children, and I lovingly welcomed his two children. We both accepted government positions under Philippine President Fidel V. Ramos; he was chairman of the Securities and Exchange Commission and I was the executive director of the Philippine Population Commission.

My sons finished high school in New York but decided to continue their studies in the Philippines to renew ties with their father. After both got married, they moved back to the United States with their spouses. They established careers on their own and raised their children without any help. Life was not easy in the United States but they proved that they could develop successful careers on their own. They are both back in the Philippines, in well-deserved positions in the hospital, running their own businesses, and raising their children.

Reflections

Unlike the American desire for independence, Filipino parents are hesitant to "push" their children out of the nest—borne out of love and a strong desire to protect them. But like birds, children only learn to do things on their own when pushed out of the nest. Our New York experience brought together positive aspects of these two cultures. While I continued to be close to my parents and respect them, I was not dependent on them. Eventually, my father understood my desire for independence. Though I was his sixth child, I was the first one to cut the "umbilical cord."

Cecile, daughter Stephanie, and husband Perfecto.

With regards to my first marriage, it was doomed to fail because we both were used to getting our way and did not have the capability to work through our differences. We were both strong-willed and when he could not get me to see it his way, out of frustration he resorted to physical violence.

While I was never going to be recognized as the model Filipina wife who is expected to be totally submissive to the husband, my second marriage proved to me that my husband and I could be equal partners.

When our ideas conflicted, I learned to accept his authority, trusting that he used his judgment for the good of the whole family. This second union produced a wonderful daughter Stephanie, who grew up in a stable home and in an environment that valued spiritual formation above all else.

These experiences taught me that God is my anchor, the One who enabled me to weather any storm. Happiness does not come from material things and accomplishments. Inner peace and lasting happiness come from an attitude of gratitude and faith in God. Total independence from my parents transformed into total dependence on God. My Filipino Catholic upbringing brought me to this place.

I have come a long way from the sheltered home I left many years ago. I have come to realize that self-reliance is not a hindrance to family ties. On the contrary, it can strengthen the family. It did mine. My children continue to receive the unconditional love from me. But unlike my parents, I let them lead independent lives with their nuclear families.

Our experience living in two cultures taught us to meld the best values from each, and this became our new reality. Our Filipino values give us the grounding to appreciate who we are. The saying that, "You will not know how to get to where you are going unless you know where you came from" rings true. Because of it, we are better equipped to succeed in our new life in the United States. We truly have the best of both worlds.

 *Cecile Joaquin Yasay graduated from St. Theresa's College in Manila. She worked for the United Nations Population Fund in New York City, and later in the Philippines as chair of the government's Population Commission. While in Hawai'i, she assisted in crafting legislation as part of Senator Donna Mercado Kim's staff. She is now involved with the ASEAN Ladies and Department of Foreign Affairs Ladies Foundations, and most recently chaired the International Bazaar Foundation which raised money for drug rehabilitation programs in the Philippines.*

Fifteen
SOLO FLIGHT
by Edna Y. Alikpala

Nothing is more daunting for a Filipina raised as a colegiala, born and bred in the relatively privileged environment of the middle class, than to be a single mother in a strange land. That was the situation I found myself in the 1980s.

I was a relatively new immigrant to Hawaiʻi and trying to make a living after leaving Manila in 1976. With an excellent educational background from high school to college at an exclusive all-girls' schools, finding a job would not be difficult, so I thought. My first job in the Philippines was with a new shipping company, a corporation owned by a family friend, receiving minimum wage pay. This working condition was unsatisfactory to my father, so using his friendship and connection with a top executive of San Miguel Corporation, I gained employment as a secretary where I worked for two years. While working, my father gave me the opportunity to enroll for evening classes at a university for more education. But within these two years, deep in my mind, I wanted to follow my dream of moving and working in the land of honey where financial success is achievable and where I can live an independent life.

Earlier, I had applied for the immigrant's third preference visa for professionals, but unfortunately it was denied. When my sister Ethel, one of the first East-West Center grantees, married Jack Ward, her marriage to an American citizen eventually opened the door for me to make this dream a reality. When she became a U.S. citizen, she petitioned for our mother's immigrant visa.

125

Edna at one of her numerous Filipino community functions.

Within several months, it was approved and my mother headed off to Hawai'i, where she eventually petitioned for her three single daughters, Lenny and Agnes residing in New York and New Jersey without permanent status, and me, still in Manila.

Subsequently, the approval of my petition for immigrant status came, but by then, I was reluctant to leave a very comfortable life with a secure job, and be separated from a relationship that was not agreeable to my parents. My ticket's final destination was New York and Hawai'i was a "stop over" for adjustment to US lifestyle as instructed by my father. Going to New York right away could be a culture shock and my sisters' residences were not able to accommodate another individual. I also had a former officemate who had moved to Hawai'i earlier and convinced me to relocate here so that I would have another family to be with to ease my homesickness if ever I experienced it. Manila was only ten hours travelling hours away. If I ever became unhappy with the new lifestyle, my father said, I could go back home!

In January 1976, I arrived in Hawai'i. After a brief rest period, first on the schedule was the intimidating process of job searching. The classified ad section was my daily guide. I had to learn to take The Bus and to use a map to find my way around to several recruitment companies to put in my application form and to go to the companies I was referred to. Unfortunately no job offers for me yet. A friend of my sister was aware of my situation, and she decided to help me by offering me a two-week part-time job at Straub Clinic where she worked as a nursing administrator in the Human Resources Department. They were dealing with the nurses' strike and there was extra work to be done. This was my chance to acclimatize myself to working in the U.S. It was an eye-opener and my top issue to deal with was communication. With my Filipino accent, I wasn't easily understood by others, even though I spoke with correct grammar. Also the work conditions were so different. For example, I was surprised that I could call the supervisory and upper management personnel by their first name. In Manila, I was trained to use titles and last names of my superior and other upper echelon management, as a sign of respect.

Before the end of the two weeks, I was informed by one of the recruitment companies that I was accepted as a clerk at Island Holidays, Ltd., one of the largest hotel and travel companies with the head office located in Waikiki. For this job referral and with my acceptance of the position, I had to pay a recruitment fee. Even with the meager salary, I felt that this could be the window for better job opportunities. Work was quite different from my experience as an executive secretary as typing financial and statistical reports was my major duty. Accuracy in typing data and figures was required.

During this time too, I passed the State of Hawai'i Civil Service examination for clerk-stenographer and secretary and my name was on the eligible list of applicants. I went to several interviews during my lunch breaks, but unfortunately I was not hired. I wasn't giving up and by luck, Toy Arre, as the deputy director in the Department of Finance, informed me that there was a vacancy in the Honolulu Fire Department. The position was for a private secretary to the Deputy Fire Chief. It was an appointed/exempt position and is co-terminus with the current Mayor's term, and not a permanent civil service job. Even with these terms, I accepted because of the salary rate and the higher level position. However, political campaigning is an additional task to this appointed position. It was at one of these meetings of the Filipino supporters that I met a person who would change the course of my life. As the saying goes, things will happen if you are at the right place and at the right time.

I was getting through a sudden breakup of my relationship with a special friend I cared for so much. We shared so many things in common, including our birthdays and I assumed this person was my soul mate, but it wasn't meant to be. Meeting this new friend and having a compatible relationship opened my heart to love again. There was that special connection with this person and my sadness and depressed state from the past breakup diminished.

After two months of being together, this happiness was interrupted when I received the sad news of the passing of my father from a heart attack. All four daughters returned immediately to Manila to bid farewell to our loving father and comfort our mother. Relatives and friends came to visit and as customary with Filipinos, they brought food. The food was appetizing and appealing, the ones I missed since I left Manila. But surprisingly, I didn't have the desire to have a bite of any of delectable arrays, especially the mouth-watering desserts. I felt that I was still coping with the stress of our sudden loss and also with the hectic schedule of coming back home, and the many activities related to the funeral service.

This happened several times so I became very suspicious of what was happening to my body. I searched for possible reasons and even though I doubted it, the only possible answer was that I was pregnant. Upon return to Honolulu, I immediately visited my physician for a check-up and blood test. No doubt about it, the blood test result was positive for pregnancy.

I can't fully describe my feelings upon receiving the news. It was an emotional day of happiness, surprise, doubt as well as fear. What do I do now, how can I provide for this child, can I have a safe pregnancy at my age and the perennial question, what will people say! After informing the soon-to-be father of our baby, his reaction was just a matter of fact, complacent acceptance. Informing my siblings took strength and courage. They said I was of age and I knew what I was doing and what I was going to get into, but they welcomed this new addition. One of the Filipino beliefs is that when one family member dies, another person is born as a replacement. This baby would replace the loss of our father!

We all agreed to spare my mother this news because she was still grieving. Being a devout Catholic with strict family traditions, the news about having an unmarried daughter with child would not be good. My brother provided me the option to consider giving birth in the Philippines with all the care and assistance available, or consider giving up the baby for adoption. None of these was acceptable to me. I was determined to give birth in Hawai'i to assure that my baby will be an American citizen. If I delivered in the Philippines, I would need to petition for the immigrant status of the baby because I was still an immigrant.

During my maternity leave from work, sick leave pay guaranteed me my regular salary. At this time, I decided I had to forego my active involvement in the civic and community organizations I belonged to. Not so much to avoid gossip, but to devote time and energy for the preparation of my child's birth. Learning to drive was a necessity too. I enrolled in driving classes, I got my driver's license, I purchased a second-hand compact car and now I was ready to drive.

Excitement grew as the days came nearer to the due date. Another hurdle needed to be overcome. My mother was scheduled to re-enter the United States as a requirement for her to maintain her immigrant status. We planned that she would go to the East Coast first and then to Hawai'i near my due date. On the day of her arrival in Hawai'i did not meet her at the airport and used work as an excuse. My sister was to drop her off at my apartment and then pick her up later in the day. This would be the time for my sister to tell her calmly of my condition and then I would come to show myself to my mother. But fate was not with us. While at my apartment, my mother decided to clean up the mess of paperwork on the table, and unfortunately found a letter from my brother in the Philippines offering help to me and my baby. My mother was shocked. I had to go home quickly with my sister to comfort and ease my mother's concern. Although it was hard for her to accept it, there was no other alternative and I can still vividly remember what she said, "If your father were alive today, he would surely have died with this news!"

April 4, 1980, Good Friday, at 3:10 p.m. Erica Jean Alikpala Cortez was born at Kaiser Hospital after eight hours of arduous labor. It was so symbolic as a gift from God to me that this birth coincided with the time of the commemoration of our Savior's death to redeem and give new life to all of us. While in the waiting room, my mother was overheard repeatedly saying, "This is unbelievable." Like all mothers, she poured out her love and care for my daughter and she was always with me to help care for her until her return to Manila.

I returned to work after a month and a half and Erica was cared by a baby sitter. Caring for my baby by myself may be tedious and tiring, especially after a full work day, but the satisfaction gained from loving my baby eased the task. There were so many motherly duties still to learn.

The added duty of campaigning was a daily challenge especially after work hours and throughout the weekend. Most of the time, I brought Erica with me while phone banking, sending mail out, or holding signs. The downside of campaigning is when your candidate loses the election. When Mayor Fasi lost his reelection bid to Eileen Anderson, all of us in appointed positions were required to tender their resignation. However, Mayor Fasi authorized the Civil Service Director to conduct civil service examinations for the appointees who desired to be on a civil service eligible list for permanent positions. I availed of this test, passed it, and waited for calls to interview. For this, I will always remember Mayor Frank Fasi with gratitude. He gave me the chance to have a stable career.

For five months—January 1981 to May 1981, I collected unemployment, and got Section 8 housing assistance and food stamps. It was a trying period but I was able to spend more quality time with my six-month old Erica. During this time, to ensure the care of Erica, I filed a child support petition through the Family Court. This was required to qualify for the program of Aid to Families with Dependent Children. Going to court and seeking this support was not acceptable to her father. DNA testing had to be done with Erica crying while a needle poked her for a blood sample, a test unlike the current practice of using a swab inside the mouth. This was my only recourse to ensure that she would be cared for financially. Judgment was in my favor and her father was ordered to pay monthly child support, though the amount was quite small. In spite of this, to this day, Erica has maintained a good relationship with her father.

Finally in June, I was hired as a clerk stenographer with the Criminal Investigation Division of the Honolulu Police Department. A year later, I was promoted to secretary with the Department of Parks and Recreation, where I eventually retired with 29 years of government service.

In 1982, Erica and I were separated for about 10 months. She travelled to the Philippines with my nephew. Heavy though this was on my heart, I allowed it so she could experience the 100 percent love and care doted on her by grandma and my sister, Lenny who had move to Manila from New York to stay with my mother. Most of all, this would allow her to experience Filipino lifestyle. I coped with this separation with long distance phone calls and looking at photographs taken of her with them in the Philippines. In August, the shocking news of the assassination of Benigno Aquino, Sr. compelled me to pick her up and return to Hawai'i. I was afraid that the event would lead to some major disaster in the Philippines, and I was anxious to get her out of there.

Erica attended Waikiki Community Center near my workplace for pre-school. When she was ready to enter school at age five, I was fortunate that she was one of ten children accepted into the kindergarten class at University Laboratory School, which had stringent rules for applicants and had an excellent academic curriculum. I participated in her activities and was one of the class moms always standing in the sidelines prepared to do anything for her and her classmates, even if I was working multiple jobs to cover increased rent, monthly preschool fees, and higher cost of living. I worked evenings and weekends in sales at Liberty House Ala Moana and Woolworth's, then at the Law Office of Graulty Ikeda and Ramirez-Uy. Throughout this duration, the support of my sister Lenny, who is now deceased, was invaluable. She took on the role of Erica's second mom and was very generous to her, both financially and with time. Besides, Ethel and her three daughters were also part of the babysitting pool whenever one was needed.

In 1998, Erica graduated from high school and she decided to pursue her college education at Pacific University in Forest Grove, Oregon. I was excited to assist in their annual luau and I travelled to be there to do haku lei, help prepare and serve food and other tasks. After graduation, she decided to settle there and I was again a single nester.

When we reach middle age, we become concerned with maintaining a healthy lifestyle. I had my annual mammography test, but after a few days, my primary care physician called to let me know he was scheduling a biopsy as a result of my mammography test. Until I received the call to see him, I was full of anxiety. Much as I did not want to hear it, he confirmed that I had Stage 1 breast cancer. I questioned why I had this dreaded disease. This was another piece of bad news that I was not ready to accept. There was no other recourse but surgery, then several sessions of radiation therapy. Erica was able to come home during her spring break. We decided to drive around the island, be like tourists and enjoy its resplendent beauty. It was a memorable time of bonding for us.

The American Cancer Society recruited me to volunteer in their Reach to Recovery program where I was assigned to visit women who were breast cancer patients for counseling and teaching them the exercise program for strengthening of their upper body and arms. Doing this was so satisfying because I was able to meet and comfort several women, just as somebody did for me after my surgery.

I've always answered the call to participate in civic and community activities ever since Ethel, during her term as president, recruited me as a member of the Filipino Women's Civic Club in 1976. I was actively involved and also became its president in 2006, and have been a member and officer of many other organizations. Hawai'i's Filipino-American community boasts of several hundreds of organizations, ranging from civic, to community, to business, religious and regional areas. Most of their goals are to assist their fellow Filipinos in Hawai'i as well as people from other respective regions. Being a member involves countless volunteer hours and financial expense with many fund raising projects, gala banquets, and pageants to attend. Erica has spent so much time with me at the meetings that she has accepted as organization members as her ohana aunties and uncles.

These organizations have contributed to developing life-long friendships, but unfortunately, enemies as well. Due to differences in opinions and perceptions, different personalities come into play, resulting in members having to cut off their relationship with each other and removing their membership from the organization. For example, there are pro-Marcos and anti-Marcos, the pro-Ariyoshi and pro-Fasi, Democrats vs. Republicans, and in recent years, the pro-rail and anti-rail factions. The elections of officers for some of these organizations can be likened to our government elections or even worse. Whichever side you belong to may make or break you. It can be a very exciting process and the community forever talks about what happened or did not happen. However, the underlying theme remains a striving for unity, and while this has proven to be elusive, hopefully one day, it will be a reality.

Significant among my involvements with Filipino community organizations is my role as the first secretary for the planning committee of the Filipino Community Center, Inc., assisting in its annual Filipino Fiesta and Parade and the annual Golf Tournaments. With Filcom Center now a reality, I am happy to know I have been a part of it from conception to inception, and recently, I have returned and volunteered to teach computer classes to our senior citizens.

Another significant volunteer opportunity was serving as the administrative assistant to Chair Elias Beniga of the Filipino Centennial Celebration Commission and its other commissioners for four years prior to 2006, the 100th anniversary of the arrival of the sakada, the Filipino sugar plantation workers. Former Governor Benjamin Cayetano established this commission to prepare for its year-long celebration. We travelled to the Big Island at the site where the first sakada landed, and also to Candon, Ilocos Sur, the first departure port in 1906.

The Filipino Association of University Women has done its duty to promote and educate the community on Filipino culture and tradition. I am happy to have led this organization as its president in 2006.

Serving the Lord is now my greatest commitment in life. With my retirement, I have devoted myself in service to Him at New Hope Oahu because I have to use what He has given me. This joy of serving is so fulfilling that no reward is expected.

Erica is now working in the financial industry and settling down with Zach, raising their son Vincent. Portland is my second home now and I visit them several times during the year because I want to be with my family to make up for the lost time when we were apart because I was busy making a living.

At the sunset of my life, there are many things I am grateful for: Erica, Vincent, and Zach who are the jewels of my crown; for my own family who have stood by me no matter what; for friends who accept me for who I am; and for the principles of truth, and integrity strongly ingrained in me so I was able to grow. My solo flight continues on its planned course and I am ready to meet the surprises and joy that will come my way.

 *Edna Alikpala retired from the City and County of Honolulu, Department of Parks and Recreation as a secretary III with 29 years of service. She volunteers weekly in several church ministries at New Hope Oahu and is actively involved in Filipino organizations. She is also is part-time baby sitter to two grandsons in Oregon from her daughter, Erica.*

Sixteen

ETIQUETTE FOR A DIVORCED WOMAN IN HAWAI'I 'S FILIPINO COMMUNITY*

by Bennette Espineli Misalucha

My Mama and Papa were married for 47 years. Until Papa suddenly died at the relatively young age of 69, my parents continued to act like teenagers at their first dance. They held hands, went on regular dates, giggled at each other's silly jokes, and listened to their stories often told, hearts held captive as if hearing these vignettes for the first time.

As a child growing up in the Philippines, I remember images of my parents at the end of a long day at our humble three-bedroom apartment in the outskirts of Cebu City. In my mind's eye, I can still see both of them in their bedroom—one would be seated by the edge of their matrimonial bed while the other may lie comfortably, propped by large pillows. It was a picture of sweet contentment. It was my parents' habit to share the highlights of their day with one another as if the sun could not set without that ritual. When I close my eyes, I can almost hear the soft muted tones from my childhood bedroom across the hall from theirs, even as I can recall their voices, punctuated by laughter that sometimes could be heard above the din of everyday household noises. Mama and Papa were each other's first boyfriend and girlfriend. More than that, they were truly each other's best friend.

The author of this essay has never read the book, Etiquette for Mistresses *by Julie Yap Daza, but admits watching the movie version and was inspired by its art form.*

Those memories of my childhood gave me solid reassurance throughout my life that the world was a safe place and that no matter what the negative circumstances might be, love would triumph in the end.

When I got married, I guess I had always assumed that such love would also be my blessing. After all, my marriage started with so much promise. Ours was a whirlwind romance, a physical attraction sealed by virtue of being intellectual equals who both understood and respected each other's drive and ambition, and who pledged to support each other throughout our careers in addition to the traditional vow to "honor and obey." Although we were almost strangers, we were sure that we "had a lifetime to share," as the strains of a favorite romantic song promised on our wedding video.

But people change. Promises can be broken. If one believes in destiny, then each of us is meant to follow different paths to complete our soul's life's lessons. After 24 years, my marriage that I thought was made in heaven, came back to earth and landed with a thud.

The demise of my marriage was the most painful period of my life. Ironically, it was also the most educational, as I achieved greater self-awareness while I sorted through the patchwork of incredible challenges, even as I courageously forced myself to question my core values and insisted on making difficult choices, ultimately deciding what to keep and what to let go from the tattered remnants of my prior life.

For refuge, I sought comfort in my faith which became my bedrock amidst trials and tribulations. My adult children and I found solace in one another. During that first year after their father left, we held tight to one another like castaways adrift in an open sea. To survive, we did not even seek answers. Instead, we resolved to cast our boat towards the hope for better times and in due time, we set our sights on healing.

I will leave out the sordid details. Suffice it to say, our divorce was the town's gossip for a while. Not surprising, since we were two people who led such public lives and somehow the local Filipino community felt it was their business to know.

But that's not what this essay is all about. After all, I'm not the first one to be divorced in this town. Neither will I be the last. But I consider my experience worth sharing. It speaks volumes about who we are, and about how our home-grown Filipino values continue to be weighed against the American norms in which we are surrounded.

How do you survive being a divorced woman in a traditional community setting that regards marriage and family as the singular social unit? What Filipino values are there that run counter to the American way of life? No one seems comfortable talking about this issue. I sure could have used some counsel while I was going through my own struggles. Casting this situation in the shadows would only perpetuate what needs to change, if it does need changing. At the very least, bringing this out in the open will stimulate some healthy discussion and hopefully, allow those going through similar experiences to realize that she is not alone.

My audience then for this essay, is the Filipina who is considering a divorce or is in the midst of the divorce process.

The dictionary defines "etiquette" as a "code of behavior that delineates expectations of decorum." Decorum suggests dignity and sense of what is becoming or appropriate for a person of good breeding."

In short, this is a primer on how to find alignment in the midst of dissonance of values, and in the end, how to discover authenticity in the process.

Lesson #1: Filipinos are uncomfortable with divorce. But remember, it's your choice; it's your life.

The Philippines is one of very few countries that do not recognize divorce. It may be attributed to the influence of the Catholic Church that dominates the rhetoric in every issue that confronts the country—whether it is political, social or civic.

Of course, there are unhappy marriages in that country or in our community. But because of our strong values about the sanctity of marriage and family, we frown upon uncoupling unhappy couples. We don't really believe in therapy either, so instead, we cling to those marital ties, no matter how flimsy these may have become over time. The stigma of divorce remains strong, the links between intermarried nuclear families so deep, it takes herculean effort to walk away from a seemingly impossible situation.

Sadly, this stubborn streak may have some unintended consequences. Filipinos, for instance, account for a high number of domestic violence cases both here and in the Philippines where domestic violence continues to be one of the most alarming and most persistent problems, with one in every five Filipino women aged fifteen to forty nine having experienced violence as reported by the National Statistics office in 2008.

In Hawai'i, in records dating 2000 to 2009, almost 25 percent of domestic violence fatalities were those of Filipino-American ancestry—the highest of all the ethnic groups.

Even for those who live in the United States where progressive laws exist and a more liberal outlook may prevail in the mainstream population, Filipinos, especially first generation ones, carry their Catholic upbringing like a second skin and are still uncomfortable about the idea of divorce. In many situations, the aggrieved party is expected to forgive and forget, no matter how grave those marital sins may be. The community elders particularly will try to convince you that it is "better to have a bad husband than to have no husband at all." True story. It happened to me. Thankfully, my own family validated my decision to divorce, and their acceptance mattered more to me than anyone else's opinion.

To my sister Filipina—it is up to you to assess whether your marriage is worth saving. This is not an easy decision. Yes, think deep and hard. Pray. Pray again. But at the end of the day, it's your choice. It's your life. If you ask a Filipino, you know what the answer will be.

Lesson #2: You will be the talk of the town. How you respond will determine how long this phase will take.

Filipinos love tsismis. And this trait is not only attributed to the women but to men too. There will be many versions of the story of how your marriage ended. All of a sudden, everyone is an expert on you. As a tidbit of gossip is passed on to the next person, it is embellished and studded with additional details, and it becomes juicier with every retelling.

You cannot take this personally. Instead, learn to deal with it with lightness and humor. Getting upset about tsismis is like fanning the flames. It is a temporary situation and trust me, people will move on to the next tsismis. It may take while, but they eventually do. Avoid people who want to share stories with you about your ex, especially those that begin with the opening statement that you "need to know." Be suspicious of those motives. More than likely, they are baiting you to see how you will respond. Do not give them that satisfaction.

And by the way, there are two schools of thought on how to act when your life's story is playing so publicly in the community. Some choose to lie low, avoiding Filipino community functions, especially those where the ex is expected to show up. Others opt to continue with their activities, hold their head high and remain in the public eye. There is no right or wrong answer. It is a preference based on your personality and life's circumstance. I chose to lie low. The tsismis mill did not need any help from me.

Lesson #3: They will try to reconcile you. Forgive them for they know not what they do.

We seem to have blinders on when it comes to our families, and forgiveness is doled out like holiday gifts without thought of consequences or gravity of the sin. As such, well-meaning friends will attempt to create situations that they hope

Bennette and children Christian and Danielle Evangelista.

will reconcile the problem couple.

Filipinos seem to have no concept of accountability in a marriage. It's not certain where this predilection comes from. One can only guess it must be from all those tele-novelas with its myriad plotline twists that Filipinos are fond of watching. Do stand your ground. These moments can be awkward, maybe even downright painful. Be firm with your friends and let them know about your intentions. What is broken cannot be unbroken especially when there is a third party involved. Forgive them. They cannot help but think that your marriage deserves a third, fourteenth, or even an umpteenth chance.

If you are consistent in your response, the community will eventually accept that there is no turning back.

Lesson #4: Filipinos have a double standard morality. Accept it and move on.

Under the Spanish regime, the idea of a double-standard morality in the Philippines started to emerge. Men could carry on discreet extramarital relations in the so-called "querida system" while women were supposed to tolerate such actions and hold themselves totally blameless, thinking that eventually, the husband would return to home and hearth.

Although there is a growing resistance to this double-standard morality, vestiges of it remain even amongst those Filipinos already living in the United States. I was shocked by the number of my Filipina women friends who did not seem fazed by the circumstances of my marriage break-up and who actually chose to defend the actions of an unhappy man. Not so surprisingly, my non-Filipino friends were more forthright and called out the actions for what they are.

I am ashamed of this side of our culture. There is nothing we can do to fight this abominable part of our past that may be deeply ingrained in our belief system. Sure, we can talk and shed light on it. But for the moment, when going through your own situation, accept it and move on.

Lesson #5: You will know who your real friends are. Treasure them.

In my younger days, when invitations to never-ending parties and community functions seemed to appear like gumdrops in a candy store, I thought that being popular was what it was all about. Dressed in the latest fashion, I reveled that my dance card was full, and my weekends were filled with events where my then husband and I could party, laugh, and meet people with like minds.

But after a divorce, do not be surprised if the pipeline to invitations slows to a trickle. Somehow the Filipino community does not know how to deal with your single blessedness. Like Noah's ark, people are used to dealing with twos.

I have always cultivated my own persona outside the realm of my marriage. I had my own standing in the community. But even I was disconcerted by the actions of others who seem to believe that I was a mere appendage to a man who now treated me differently.

Thank heavens for true and authentic friends who continue to validate my worth as an individual. This experience will truly separate the grain from the chaff. Treasure those friends that stay true to you. They have their weight in gold. Sadly, I lost some friends during the divorce. I continue to grieve for those losses.

Lesson #6: Find your center and embrace who you are.

I know it's easier said than done, but as you transition into the new normal, find something that will redefine who you are. Dig deep into your soul and determine what makes you happy and fulfilled. It may take some trial and error to uncover the activities that will make your heart soar, but surely it is worth the discovery.

For me, writing became my salvation. It was a talent that got waylaid as I spent many years in the corporate world where my ode to the written word often came in the form of technical instructions on banking procedures.

But as I reconnected with the pleasure of stringing words together, I began to enjoy the joyous exercise of bringing life to ideas that were held once held captive in my mind and needed to see the light of day. I went back to my roots in media and found my footing as the managing editor of a community paper. I finally heard my own voice and in so doing, helped others find theirs as well.

I count myself blessed that I found my true calling.

Lesson #7: Life is a Journey. Be patient.

Life is a journey and we need to be patient in seeing our individual journeys through. There will be good days when the horizon seems to signal nothing but bright skies ahead. But there will be dark moments too, days when you feel alone. But divorce is not the end of the world, and you will weather this storm.

Filipinos are well known to be as resilient as the bamboo. We could be hammered by the strongest typhoon to hit the earth but we still manage to rebuild our lives with eternal optimism and the countenance of a grateful heart.

This trait has served us well when we Filipinos immigrated to America as part of the great diaspora. We never feel sorry for ourselves. No matter our socio-economic situations, we are still able to smile. In America, when confronted with problems, we work even harder, burying our emotions until we can bounce back.

That's just who we are. Like the proverbial phoenix, the indomitable Filipino human spirit rises again and again, against all odds, refusing to let anything or anyone get us down. We are the survivors. Hang on to that resilience. These strong values will get you through the darkest times.

It has been six years since my marriage ended and I can honestly say I am happy and content with my life. Faith in my Heavenly Father has kept me grounded and has enabled me to look at trials from a new perspective. It is a chance to grow. In my heart, I have forgiven those that may have wronged me, even as I have asked for forgiveness in my prayers for those that I have wronged. My children and I have never been closer and the family crisis has only served to cement the ties that bind. Mama now lives in the Philippines but I am constantly in touch with her and the rest of my four siblings who are spread out between Texas, Utah, Baguio, and Manila. I choose to lead a much quieter but more authentic life nowadays. I love staying home on weekends, quietly reading, watching movies or puttering in my garden, maybe even occasionally getting together with choice friends. I am still involved in the Filipino community but I carefully choose how to spend my time. I am a living proof that a divorced Filipina, while not ideal, does not need to choose between her own people's values and her new-found freedom. Mama and Papa would have been proud.

And yes, despite of what I have gone through, my original worldview remains the same. I still believe in love and I still believe that love will triumph in the end.

 *Bennette Espineli Misalucha is a former television reporter/anchor/producer in Cebu, Philippines and in Hawai'i. She has held leadership roles in banking, government relations, and community engagement sectors throughout her career. She is currently the managing editor of the Filipino newspaper,* Fil-Am Courier, *published in Honolulu.*

Seventeen
GOING THE OTHER WAY
by Grace Manio

I have never imagined, even in my wildest dreams, that my non-conformist mindset, sometimes source of abrasion, would become a major life changer. As a child, I always got in a lot of trouble for asking too many questions and doing the opposite of what I was told and expected to do. I am a first-born child and a girl. In most Asian cultures, firstborns are supposed to be the example, the leader, the one that is like the second parent to the rest of the children in the household. A female child is also told to be gracious, well mannered, and proper in her ways. I totally do not fit the description.

My father was in the Philippine Air Force, a very distinguished, well decorated, and very feared military officer during the martial law days. He was a man of few words but very quick to act. He was a disciplinarian, an intellectual, the Corps Commander when he was in the Philippine Military Academy. You can imagine the times that I received "correction" and they were many. I never really had much interaction with him. I remember mostly being with him during dinners and during "correction time."

My mother was an accountant when we lived in Manila. She was the first to graduate from college in her family, who raised animals and tended a small farm. She was ambitious and wanted to leave her agricultural roots in Pampanga to be the first one to be part of the corporate world. I believe that I got my non-conformist mindset from her, although as time went on, I think she conceded and started to conform. My aunt, her sister, told me a story about my mother when she was three years old during the Japanese occupation of the Philippines. My mother put her whole family's life in danger. They were evacuating and she was asking for water. They gave her water in a coconut shell but she refused. She kept crying because she wanted to drink from a cup and not from the coconut shell. Even at an early age, she knew what she wanted and went for it.

She fell in love with my father, head over heals. He was charismatic, but a very difficult man. She often kissed my father although he couldn't stand public displays of affection. She was the perfect hostess whenever we had parties attended by other military officers and their families; we were living in an "officer housing" unit at what was then Nichols Air Base. She was forced to abandon her career in finance because my father forbade her to work. She was only to take care of the household and the children. I often heard arguments, sometimes very heated ones because my mother wanted a career outside the home. I felt that there was something wrong with their relationship but I was too young and too busy getting into trouble.

How much trouble can an elementary school girl get into? Well, for starters, I could never keep my Catholic school uniform clean because I played rough in the dirt even before the school bell rang. I talked back to my second grade teacher because she said that the homework I turned in was unacceptable. I drew myself in a ballerina tutu with the peace symbol on my forehead. It was 1973. I saw it on TV a lot. There was always something in me that needed to be expressed, but that was not encouraged. "Children were seen and not heard," my father used to say.

In 1975, my father died of cancer of the lungs. He was a three-pack-a-day smoker and was always flying military airplanes and helicopters. I sensed something was troubling him but he never spoke about it. He was only thirty-four years old. His death brought out many emotions I felt but had a hard time describing and understanding. I feared him but also longed for him. He was mysterious and demanded perfection. I was nine and my two younger sisters couldn't really understand what was going on.

My mother remarried three years later. I believe that she married my stepfather for pragmatic reasons. He was kind, very patient, and supportive. He was much nicer than my father. He would do things with us that made me feel a bit normal. He took us to the park and to the movies. He smiled more and joked a lot. Although she remarried, I suspect that my mother's real love is still my father because she doesn't have that sparkle in her eyes when she speaks to my stepdad. Her eyes sparkled when she was with my father. My stepdad was nurturing but not mysterious. He showered my mother with affection. My mother often told him to be more discreet. They must have had some form of intimacy because my brother was born in 1979. We welcomed him and he became the apple of my mother's eye.

My mother became like my father. She continued the strict upbringing, using an achievement-oriented point system in our household. I was a senior in college when she told us that we were migrating to the United States. After graduating from the University of Santo Tomas with a degree in Business Administration and after the EDSA revolution, we left. I went to Guam first to visit family there. I purposely asked to go there instead of California where the rest of my family settled. I was shocked when my mother said yes. I wanted to escape the "rules." I was already 20 years old and wanted to start living my "non-conformist" life so I joined the United States Navy. My parents were upset, but I wanted my freedom. My sister also wanted to leave so she got a scholarship to Penn State in the East Coast and graduated from there. My mother, at this time, was starting to realize that her children were rapidly assimilating the values and ideologies of their new country, the United States. The two other siblings I have were still in high school and elementary. My mother was desperately trying to control their social lives and their peer groups. It was hard. There were disagreements and tears.

Despite all these things that somewhat challenged the values that formed our youth, all four of us were able to maintain our respect for our parents. We never cursed or disrespected our mother, not like some of the other young people that we knew that were natural-born Americans. We reasoned with her. We disagreed with her, but she was still our mother. I knew that some of my younger brother's schoolmates rebelled. He would sometimes tell us stories about the fights that these schoolmates would have with their families. He told us that they sometimes would tease him about his "Filipino ways" because he never talked bad about his parents. Was it because of the Filipino value of respecting our parents and elders that made the difference? Or was it the fear of disappointing and hurting our mother? Or maybe both.

It was in 1988, just a few months after boot camp that I met and married my husband. He was in Naval Aviation. I don't get attracted to civilians. I really didn't realize this till later that my longing for my real father strongly influenced my preference of military men. It was the familiarity of the lifestyle and the mystery of men in uniform. Tony was well liked by my family because he, too, was charismatic. Tony was the life of the party. He was a handsome Latino man that confidently showed his charm. He knew how to make my mother smile. She rarely smiled. She didn't smile even in her photos. We had two children, Mia and Carlo. They are almost seven years apart because we were both in the military and had many deployments.

I started to buy into conformity because of my children. I left the military because being a dual military family was causing a strain in our marriage. I sacrificed my career so I could be with the children. It's funny how history can repeat itself. My mother had to stop being an accountant to become a full-time homemaker. The difference between us is that she hated having to give up her career, while I enjoyed doing so. I became "Suzie, the Homemaker." The expressive side of me became a cook, a soccer mom who sometimes successfully baked cookies and banana bread.

I thought, at the time, that conforming wasn't too bad. Little did I know that in becoming a homemaker, I became very unattractive to my husband. He carried on affairs with other women. I knew they were there but I chose to keep quiet and to bear the ugly truth. I couldn't let my family know about his cheating ways because my mother loved him. To her, Tony could do no wrong. As my children got older, my oldest child started asking questions, like, why was their Dad always coming home late or why was I crying sometimes? I covered up a lot of the pain because, given my family's achievement-oriented point system, it would be a disgrace to fail.

I became like my mother who did all the parenting. I taught my children what I learned from my parents, the same lessons that I rebelled against quietly when I was growing up. I realized that my mother was strict because she wanted us to focus on our academics. She didn't even allow me to have any suitors until I was a senior in college. Her strong work ethic helped me to endure boot camp and became a really good sailor. The value of keeping the family together and intact was first and foremost in her eyes. I couldn't tell her I was suffering. I couldn't tell her that my daughter begged me one day to consider leaving because she saw her father kissing another woman outside our home when I was out of town. I didn't know how to fight for myself. I hid everything when we would see my family. We often visited my parents because we were stationed in California for 11 years. My mother often expected us to spend most of our holidays with them. Tony's family was so troubled that he really didn't want to be around them.

It was on the twelfth year of our marriage when we left California and moved to Hawaiʻi. My mother cried a lot at the airport. I knew it was painful. I didn't think I could leave her either. I also thought that Tony and I could fix what's broken. Maybe paradise could rekindle the fire that we once had.

I was wrong. I filed for divorce and I became the official black sheep of the family. The distance from my mother helped me decide to get divorced. I said to myself that this was the only way. If I asked her, she would have convinced me or maybe even ordered me to stay married. No one divorces in our family. I am the first! My mother was furious with me. Little did I know that what I would do in two years after the divorce, would earn me another name.

Before the divorce, I decided to go back to the military. In 1999, I joined the Navy Reserves. I became a Religious Programs Specialist or a Chaplain's assistant. I wanted to have some security. I didn't want to lose all my military benefits. It was my plan to stabilize and keep the familiar. The divorce was finalized the following year. The new millennium brought a lot of hope for me to rebuild my life and perhaps really be me again. I didn't even know at that time who "me again" was because I had been conforming for a long time.

My focus was totally on my two children and helping them cope with the divorce. I was thirty four and a single parent. I was not dating and was not interested in anyone. My civilian job as the Director of Religious Education for the Marine Corps Base and my other position as an enlisted Petty Officer in the Navy Reserves kept me busy. As a Petty Officer Second Class, I was considered a junior non-commissioned officer, an E-5. In the corporate world, I would be considered a junior executive and in management.

One day, the chaplain called me into his office and told me that he needed me to start a volunteer program involving single marines and sailors for the youth program. He wanted me to recruit and make a speech at every service that weekend. I did. I also set up a sign-up area for those who wanted to volunteer. Many that signed up that day. One of them was a young, 19-year-old Filipino marine.

"Can you please tell me your name, Lance Corporal?" I asked him.

"It's Ramses Manio, ma'am," he replied.

"Ramses? Like the Egyptian Pharaoh?" I asked him again.

"Yes, Ma'am," was the reply.

I looked up. He was staring at me. It was piercing and I felt uncomfortable. I told him to sign the form and show up for orientation the following week. We had to train the volunteers on the protocol and how to work with the youth. Lance Corporal Manio was always there. He never missed any volunteer opportunity. He was helpful, and many of the kids liked him. My daughter, who was 12 at that time, even had a crush on him. She said, "He is cute." I considered him one of the best volunteers for that program. The only time he would miss coming to sessions was when he was deployed. He often sent me early notification when that happened. He also sent me postcards from the places where he was deployed. He always remembered me on my birthday. In the two years since he started volunteering, he gave me Christmas presents. "What a nice young man," I thought to myself.

Christmas 2000 came and my youngest sister and cousin visited me. They were both asking me to find someone cute to chaperone them around. The only person that came to my mind was Lance Corporal Manio. I hesitated at first because fraternization was frowned upon in the military. I was an E-5 and he was an E-3 at the time. I thought maybe it's okay since I am not the one that he will be chaperoning around. My daughter thought that it was a good idea so they convinced me to ask him if would go out with them. I asked him and he said yes. Off they went. Every time I asked them how everything was going, my cousin and my sister would ask me if I thought Ramses was gay.

"Gay? Why?" I asked. They told me that he never showed any clue about my cousin flirting with him openly. They

153

also told me that he asked a lot of questions about me.

"Me? What kind of questions?" I inquired. He asked them about my likes and dislikes and what I am interested in. My younger sister jokingly told me that she thought he had a serious crush on me. "Perish the thought!" I told her. It was absurd and totally unlikely. I explained to them that he was quite shy but loved to be helpful. He was just doing this as a favor. My sister still insisted that he has special feelings for me but I totally dismissed it. How can a 21-year-old have special feelings for a 35-year-old single parent? He was even younger than my youngest brother. Besides, my own daughter had a crush on him.

The tragedy of September 11, 2001, the day that shook the very foundations of our country, happened. I got a phone call. It was Lance Corporal Manio. He was getting ready to be shipped out. He said he might be leaving in a day. They were on standby. I told him it was nice that he called me but asked him if he called his family in California. He said he didn't yet because he called me first. I was a bit perplexed but dismissed any thoughts. I told him that I was also getting called in for active duty but was staying here in Hawai'i as a replacement for the ones leaving to go to the theater of operations. After we hung up, I felt something strange. Why was I the first person he called? Was it, perhaps, because I was the only older Filipina woman that he knew here in Hawai'i? Maybe I was like the ate (older sister).

The following month was such a blur because of all the things that 911 brought about; duties and chaos followed the event. One day, I received a call from the DSN line, the phone line that can only take official military calls. I was at the chapel office. I picked up the phone and it was him.

"Lance Corporal, how are you? Is everything okay? You are calling me on the DSN line."

He paused for a while, "I just wanted to hear your voice, Petty Officer," he answered.

Ramses and Grace Manio.

"Ok, well you shouldn't be calling me on this line. You know that this is only for official business. But I am glad you are okay." Then I hung up. My thoughts went back to the time my sister said that he might have a serious crush on me. I thought that it couldn't be because of our 15-year gap. Totally impossible!

Spring of 2002 came and he returned. This time, he went to see me in person. He asked if he could take me out to lunch. He said he needed advice. I felt bad because I hung up on him when he called me on the DSN line so I said yes. I told him to meet me at the back gate of the base after my physical training. We went to Maui Tacos in Kailua. For the first time, I saw him in civilian clothes. I was still in my Navy-issued exercise gear.

"Thank you for accepting my invitation, Petty Officer," he said as he pulled out my chair so I can sit.

"It's okay, Lance Corporal. You said you need advice."

"Please call me Ram and can I please call you Grace? We are not in uniform," he replied.

My heart started to beat faster and my thoughts were racing. What was he going to tell me? He started talking about this woman that he liked. He was afraid of getting rejected because the situation was unique. "I like you a lot, Grace. I have always liked you since I saw you make that announcement for volunteers. That is why I volunteered."

I felt the room spin; it was like I was in the twilight zone. I know that it sounds so corny but that is how I really felt. My mind couldn't accept what I just heard. I didn't know how to respond so I laughed. I knew that I hurt his feelings. "Ram, I am flattered but I really don't know what to say. You are a very nice young man with so much future ahead of you. You are probably confused about all this because you miss your family in California." I couldn't even look at him.

"I know that this is a shock, Grace, but I am serious. I may be young but I have been through a lot in my life so I know who I want to be with," he responded. I felt like I was in a movie or a trick reality show.

Months passed after that day at Maui Tacos in Kailua. He didn't show up to volunteer anymore. The chaplain told me to set up a dinner to thank all the volunteers. I sent out invitations to everyone, including one to him. I found myself thinking of our last conversation. I realized I missed him a lot. "What! Wait! What am I thinking? What am I feeling?" I know that I am a non-conformist by nature but now I am a cougar! A non-conforming cougar? It's crazy! How do I tell my children? How do I tell my mother? Remember her? My mother who ruled with an iron fist and who adhered to all the norms and traditions of the Filipino culture?

But to make a long story short, we got married secretly on September 1, 2002. My children understood but not my mother. She threatened to disown me and maybe even to disinherit me. It was painful because finally I have a husband that loves me and adores me regardless of our 15-year gap; he is faithful to me and is a friend to my children. She forbade me to tell any of our relatives that I married again and that I married a young man at that. She made me feel that I violated God's laws.

It took a while before she accepted my husband but she finally did. She doesn't adore him like she did Tony, but at least she invites Ram now to our home in California. It's been almost 14 years. Our love works because we have so much in common. The Filipino culture helps us make our relationship work despite our age difference. The values that he has are the values that I have. We are both Kapampangan. This is also a factor in helping my mother accept him because of the Pampanga connection.

Do I consider myself a Pinay that kept tradition or someone that left them behind? I can say I have done both. I can never forget the values that my mother instilled in me so I can succeed. But I also had to free myself from the ties that bound me before or I couldn't be me—a non-conformist woman who found freedom to be who she is and to love again despite the odds.

 *Grace Manio is a graduate of Business Administration from the University of Santo Tomas in Manila. She migrated to the U.S. after the EDSA revolution and joined the United States Navy. She is the mother of four and is blessed with three grandchildren. She lives in Makakilo, Hawai'i with her husband Ramses.*

Eighteen
ARISING FROM THE ASHES
by Fe Lucero Baran

I am 74 years old, born and raised in Cebu, Philippines. Of dual citizenship, I have lived in California for over 40 years. I lost Nick, my husband of 42 years, four years ago, so quickly, so suddenly. No, not in my arms. He was gone while I was away; snatched by a cardiopulmonary arrest. His epitaph reads: Nicholas Michael Baran—Rudawka, Poland, 1939; Danville, California, 2012. "For lasting memory and everlasting life."

Ashes to Ashes

To everyone but me, it was an ordinary day in 2012, a warm sunny summer Sunday, as is usual in Los Angeles, California. This particular day will forever lurk in the recesses of my memory as an episode I don't relish revisiting. The hazy atmosphere enveloped an unmoving cruise ship from Puerto Vallarta and Cabo San Lucas docked on the pier spent from a week of often loud gaiety of cruisers. The Tien family, Taiwanese friends residing in San Ramon, CA, had invited Nick and me to join them, but Nick had no appetite for a cruise. He was preoccupied with final retirement papers; so, on this sunny Sunday morning in August, without him, we slowly spilled out to the parking lot with our luggage. Gone was the excitement of the departure a week ago, just the calm and relieved feeling of arriving safely and the subtle exhaustion one often feels at the end of vacation.

We quietly drove back through Los Angeles and then along the highway north. The last time I touched base with

Nick was Friday, as my phone was off to save the battery during travel, and I was anxious to return to the normalcy of our life. As we drove past Bakersfield, which was less than the halfway point of the 350-mile trip, Cat, my youngest daughter called. She was happy I was back, and I was also happy to be back and relieved, but she carried foreboding news: Dad hadn't answered his phone since yesterday, Saturday.

My heart skipped a beat; he had not answered my last call from Los Angeles either. To not return calls was out of character for him. Last Friday, on the return voyage from Mexico, I couldn't sleep well. This had better be a joke, Nick. It would be so out of character, nonetheless. Upon my scheduled arrival, he would have finished many garden or household projects, gone to Costco, and cleaned the house. As the oatmeal expert, he would have made breakfast with fresh blueberries, fresh orange juice, and even his favorite sliced tomato. There would definitely be freshly brewed coffee. Did he go out with friends? But why not answer phone calls or text messages? It was extremely out of character. This had better be a joke, Nick!

Jesus, Mary, and Joseph, I give you my heart and my soul. Jesus, Mary and Joseph, assist me in my last agony. Even from my youth, I have always said this particular prayer. Prayer, in general, was an integral part of my Filipino family life when we prayed the rosary every evening and went to mass together. However, this particular prayer subconsciously conditioned me to the idea of death and should have prepared me for the inevitable. Furthermore, at my retirement two years prior to Nick's, I had included Nick in this prayer. Jesus, Mary, and Joseph, I pray this for Nick, too. It had better be a big joke, Nick!

Driving home after a long trip usually feels like it goes faster probably because the way looks so familiar. This time, however, it felt like an eternity and everything was a blur as I sat silent in the car without saying anything about Nick to the others. I thought of how on Friday as we returned along the

159

waves from Mexico, I could not sleep. Did something change in my life and somehow I had felt it?

Finally, we arrived by early afternoon and the Tiens dropped me off in Danville, a ten-minute detour from their San Ramon residence. Over the second half of the car ride, my anxiety had silently multiplied. My heart was now pounding. I could feel it in my head. Despite my disorientation, I noticed the house was beautiful. The portion of grass in front was green and fresh even though the temperature was probably in the 90s. The meandering brook of salt and pepper tiny pebbles curved like a welcoming ribbon from the doorway to the mailbox at the end of the yard. The serenity of the yard mirrored the serenity of our lives at that time, as we were just settling into our lives of retirement. But then a tell-tale sign. If Nick had gone out with friends would he have done so overnight? His favorite Saturday edition of the Financial Times was abandoned on the driveway. It's the first thing he would pick up before preparing our oatmeal breakfast, the fresh orange juice, the blueberries and tomato, and the freshly-brewed coffee. I took the suitcase handed to me and made an effort to holler happily, "Good bye. Don't worry about waiting. I will talk to you later. Thanks."

I didn't notice anything anymore. I didn't see the two neatly trained black pines guarding the entrance to the house, the well-proportioned bay window in the living room that Nick loved, nor the muted blue-green front door. I turned the key to let me in and felt the cool air inside as I dropped my suitcase in the hallway and hollered: "Nick, where are you?"

He would have heard me right away if he were in the kitchen or living room or even in the bedrooms of our four-bedroom, one-story bungalow. The first room to my right in the second hallway was the computer room. "Hey, Nick!" The door was wide open. Light was filtering through the window screen. There he was.

His swivel chair cradled him, turned toward the door away from the computer. I ran toward him and stopped. His

160

head was tilted backward toward his right on the high-backed chair. His right arm hung limp. His fingers touched the wooden floor. His left arm, also limp, was next to the left armrest. Gingerly feeling his face, I shuddered; his skin was cold and clammy. I tried to close his unseeing eyes, but no, I couldn't. They were lifeless and so was he. Yet so relaxed and peaceful, there was no sign of struggle. To the unsuspecting observer, Nick had no physical condition. He walked everyday and lifted weights recording his regimen faithfully in pads of yellow paper. He had the six-foot physique of a trim and handsome man looking much younger than many at 73.

In the Philippines, there is always someone in the house; I would have hollered for help. In the United States, I learned early on to call 911. Danville is a small city of around 40,000 people and the fire department and police are nearby and always at hand. My oldest daughter's best friend from childhood, Eleni, was right there, too. I don't remember calling anybody except 911, but my kitchen was filled with neighbors. Everything was surreal, numbing, catatonic. Did I call my three daughters? Coco, my oldest, was home in Los Angeles with her husband and three young children. Jojo, in San Luis Obispo, was just starting her first year at Central Coast Pathology. Cat, my youngest, was also in her first year as physician assistant at the Greater Baltimore Medical Center. No, now I recall, I did not. Cat called me again after the police arrived. Then she called Jojo and Coco to tell them the news that they secretly dreaded could be true. We all have our deaths and our comprehension of them. This one was incomprehensible for all who knew Nick, but for me, annihilating.

Grief

Grief in itself is so personal. We have several experiences of loss varying from a misplaced pair of earrings, an important purse, or a precious friend, which make us sad, but the loss of a loved one, a partner for decades, is a living death by a thousand cuts. Ancient Greeks believed that we spend all our lives

161

looking for "our half" and we would not be whole and happy until we find him or her. What happens now when you lose him? What about death then? Where do the dead go? Is there really another dimension more perfect than the perfect world we try to achieve in life? Can I convince myself that dolce far niente, the joy of doing nothing, is actually his incomprehensible death, not the perfect retirement he had envisioned?

As Catholics, especially in the Philippines, we desire a good death, not as heroes dying in wars nor victims of violence but as ordinary people dying peacefully with family around praying. My favorite cellist, Yoyo Ma, serenaded his father playing Bach in his final hours. Except for the silent computer, there was no music playing for Nick. And then there was me, me alone.

Fortunately for Nick and me, the policeman in attendance thoughtfully asked if there was a pastor or priest he could contact, and he called Father Ray, our parish priest at St. Joan of Arc, who came immediately. A policeman would seem like an odd presence in the Philippines at a death bed, nonetheless, he and the priest would begin a series of consolation that at that time I felt was for Nick, but that I needed so much then but didn't realize until later. When he arrived, Father Ray knew Nick was already dead. He drew back the sheet covering his face. He and I prayed. He reassured me Nick was still there. Even now, I still hope Nick's spirit was indeed lingering to have seen his forehead anointed with Holy Oil. I hope he was still there to hear the prayer asking God to pardon his sins and receive his soul and that he would soon see God face to face in all eternity.

From family to community, Filipinos are traditionally famous in their extended family and community celebrations. Think of town fiestas where everyone, even strangers and long-lost friends are welcome to dine and watch the procession of the patron saint and the devotees. Similarly, in death, everyone is welcome to pray, to console the living, and celebrate life with hope for the future. In particular, there's the possibly week-long wake when prayers are said, gifts are brought and people share meals or snacks. Nick, the police, and Father Ray left me in the hands of a collection of shocked neighbors and close friends, who brought food and bided their time until Jojo, my middle daughter arrived from San Luis Obispo. In our simplified and perhaps sanitized life in Danville, California, and the circumstance of Nick's sudden death, we had no wake, not even private viewing. I decided to have his body cremated and not embalmed. He was dressed in his favorite Lucky blue jeans, his favorite dusty pink Faconnable linen shirt, and his favorite pair of Allen Edmonds shoes, although only our family appreciated it, as we had no open casket.

Nick's funeral was grand in a low-key manner. The program read: Order of Christian Burial for Nicholas Baran. Instead of Yoyo Ma, we had two cantors singing and leading, a pianist on a grand piano, and a tender violinist playing music inspiring meditation and sweet sorrow as in Schubert's Ave Maria and inspiring hope in a wondrously powerful and loving God as in hymns like Be Not Afraid, How Great Thou Art, Song of Farewell, and Prayer of St. Francis. "For it is in dying that we are born to eternal life," wrote St. Francis of Assisi. This time, it wasn't just Fr. Ray and me praying over Nick. Our dear old friend Father James, who like us all could not comprehend Nick's death, drove down from the North. There were friends and parishioners praying and singing in church. Nick's casket, covered with a sheet of white silk, was in full view at the foot of the altar. With Fr. Ray and Fr. James concelebrating the mass, the homily and readings affirmed not only the exemplary life Nick lived but also our longing to be with a loving God whose supreme desire is for us to live forever. Cat read Nick's letter to the Polish government requesting dual citizenship indicating his history and the fact that he did not leave Poland of his own will but was one of a dozen children rescued from Siberia due to the exigencies of war. Coco then read some lines from Song of Songs:

My beloved is like a gazelle

There he stands behind our wall…

See! The winter is past…

Arise, come…my beautiful one, come with me.

Within a few days after Nick's death, all the guests had left. The inurnment was simple and very private. With all the arrangements in order to pick up the urn containing Nick's ashes, we drove him to the Oakland Cathedral of Jesus the Light. Located on Merritt Lake, the modern wooden and glass edifice is inspiring, with the mausoleum located underneath the church. With the church above, one can even attend mass and pray at the tabernacle or pray quietly in the mausoleum.

Father James was kind enough to preside also at the inurnment and we prayed with him before the urn was placed in the niche, an enclosed glass shelf adorned with tiny metal flowers, enhanced by a grand stained glass window bearing the image of St. Matthew. In the middle of the bay was a bench I sat on to meditate and pray, viewing Nick's reddish orange Oriental urn. He would approve—an offering of ashes to be renewed by the Holy Spirit one day. The peace and quiet in the columbarium was in sympathy with our prayers. May you rest in peace, Nick. May your ashes rekindle in all eternity at the end of time.

We walked out of the mausoleum and into the portico. In front of the stairs, I stood before a huge replica of Michelangelo's Pieta. It was exactly as I found Nick in his computer chair. Instead of the flowing mantle hiding Mary's arms, his computer chair had cradled him. The Christ looked abandoned but he didn't look like one who had just been crucified. He was certainly already looking like the glorified Christ resting. I felt a renewal of pity and awe for Mary. What is this grieving Mother trying to tell me? In the Presentation of Jesus at the Temple, Simeon predicted to Mary: …"and a sword shall pierce your heart." Her heart must have been pierced many times even as one witnesses the Stations of the Cross. At the point of his death, I hope Nick saw Mary's gentle sorrow in her beautiful, young face.

Guilt, Self-Pity, and Anxiety

They say, after the funeral when company leaves, one begins the process of mourning, a long process for me of comprehending the reasons for my grief. However, with everybody gone, I felt there was nothing of importance any more, and I was engulfed in my own thoughts. I wonder if guilt is grief's cousin. It was certainly closer than that for me. Guilt for having gone on a vacation without Nick and coming home finding him dead. With guilt, it seems, comes anxiety. So much so that I was even afraid of the idea that Nick might appear to visit me. What would I say? Forgive me for not being there for you? I am sorry, I could have paid more attention to you before my trip?

Without any discussion, the Tien family certainly understood these feelings. They invited me to stay in their house and I did for one month, going there for dinner and leaving early morning. Where could I go? I went to church every morning and sat there not praying. "Where else can we go, Lord? You have the word of everlasting life." I didn't think of it then. I was just there. And Nick was gone.

Rising from the Ashes

The tasty and nutritious Taiwanese cooking of the Tiens certainly did me a lot of good. I didn't realize it then. They were also a happy family who enjoyed laughter and togetherness. I needed the happy company. In addition, I intuitively looked for a place to exercise. The Danville Senior Center was more than perfect, as everything in Danville seems to be. St. Thomas Aquinas who taught the importance of taking care of physical conditions to cure spiritual ones must have nudged me. I finally got inspired too to join the Grief Support group in the parish. We were supposed to write a letter to our lost loved one to see

165

if we still feel the same way after the sessions. "I'm sorry Nick for having left you alone." But there I was alone too.

In the Philippines, there is always someone in the house—a family member in the ancestral home, faithful helpers in-house, and neighbors one sees everyday outside the window. In my support group there was a Filipino, Rudy, whose wife died in the shower. Ironically, a bath or a shower alleviates stress and heals the spirit, in my experience. However, Rudy and I inherited common difficulties. His wife took care of the household especially finances. He didn't know where documents were filed. Similarly, I had not even balanced a check book in my life with Nick. Then Nick wasn't around to do it for me. Ah, the face of self-pity. We were certainly poor ones. The support group did not make me all whole when we parted ways. I had neither the desire for company nor new relationships. I became more anxious about my finances and was either too trusting or paranoid even with professionals that I met.

Pampering myself, I had my hair cut as short as I had ever worn it since I was a child. I didn't like it. Nothing in my first year helped except for calls and visits from my daughters, especially Jojo who had moved to San Luis Obispo, three hours by car from Danville.

At last, year one without Nick ended. In her book, *A Widow's Memoir*, Joyce Carol Oates says, "On the first anniversary of her husband's death, the widow should think I kept myself alive." I congratulated myself. The second year my hair was colored dark blond. I wasn't sure about my looks. Because I couldn't continue living alone, I sold my house in Danville, moved into our house in Pismo Beach, and I went on a pilgrimage to the Holy Land. I should have felt like a triple-crown winner in a horse race, like Seabiscuit, with garlands of roses around my neck. In the meantime, my hair started losing the golden streaks. And now in my fourth year, my hair has almost completely gone back to the normal black, except it is

166

trying to go salt-and- pepper just like the gravel in my Danville home.

Convinced that my Filipino cultural background and my Catholic faith enabled me to cope with the devastating loss of my husband Nick, I wish that my children, who came together so profoundly to mourn our loss, would understand and remember that as a Filipina, I will have left them a lifetime of cultural and spiritual legacy. Although one cannot escape generational differences and the profound shift showing that a third of children raised in faith-filled families stop practicing their faith and parental cultural values after high school, I hope that my children, like the mythical phoenix, will in their lifetime, rise up glorious and magnificent in their existing multicultural life.

Fe Baran is a graduate of St. Theresa's College in Cebu City and the University of California, Los Angeles. She is certified in Teaching English as a Second Language (TESL). Fe lives in Pismo Beach, California.

Nineteen
KALIGTASAN (SALVATION)
by Jeramae Marcellano

I clearly remember as if it was just yesterday, the forceful, constant sound of an oxygen machine that filled the atmosphere of my aunt's shared hospital room. She had been diagnosed with an advanced stage of breast cancer in 2010 and within two years, her health had quickly deteriorated. I cannot forget her expressionless face, which she sometimes forcefully moved in order to respond. My sisters and I surrounded her bed, singing hymnal songs to help comfort and ease her pain. I even tried to alleviate some of her pain by massaging her hand and providing comfort in any way possible.

I remember asking her, "Tita, anong masakit? (What hurts?) Gusto mo ba tawagin ko yung nurse mo? (Do you want me to call your nurse?) Sandali lang ha? (Just hang in there, ok?)" With difficulty, she responded with a simple, "Thank you," and those were the last words that I heard from her before she ultimately became unresponsive and passed on.

This was my first time to experience dealing with a death of a loved one and I was really terrified. My aunt was my mother's sister and had lived with us for about five years. No one expected that someone so close to our family would have been very ill and most especially die because of cancer. A few questions that I remember asking myself were, "What do we do now? How are we even supposed to plan for her funeral? How do they even perform funeral services in America?" With all the uncertainties and fear that came along in learning how to deal with a dying person, one thing was certain. My aunt's death helped me to reflect on what I learned when my parents taught

168

me the grace of salvation or what is also termed in Tag¡ kaligtasan. I am convinced that despite her struggle with cancer and shortcomings in life, my aunt received salvation while she was still alive and that I will be seeing her again in heaven.

Throughout my lifetime, I have experienced dealing with death through a family friend or distant relatives. I was never the type of person who would look into a casket to say my parting words nor have I ever been in a situation where I had to be a part of planning for a funeral service. I used to always fear death. Perhaps, I was not knowledgeable about the concept of death and did not know what to expect. Yet, when I reflect back to this time, I think, as a natural consequence of being human, I was simply in denial.

In the Philippines, it is customary to have funeral services held at home. I recall attending wake services held in the house of a deceased individual while other similar services would be conducted in a funeral home. The coffin was usually placed either outside, covered with a tent, or in the living room, surrounded by funeral lights with many different flower arrangements. Typically, the wake is held 24 hours every day and guests are welcome to visit at any time. It is also a Filipino tradition to have lamayan or paglalamay. This is when friends and family would stay up the whole night, playing music, games, gambling, or to be the "midnight watch," at least, this is what I was told it was. I also remember that there was usually a procession before the final funeral service and inurnment. Dressed in black, family and friends would walk while following the hearse on its way to the cemetery.

The Philippines is also noted for its Catholic practices with certain customs, rituals, and practices. In addition, there are countless superstitions, also known as pamanhiin. For instance, when I was about six years old, when one of our distant relatives passed away, the old folks lola (grandmother) and lolo (grandfather) required each child to be passed back and forth atop the casket before it was lowered into the grave.

According to my grandmother, this is usually done for the children so that the spirit of the dead would not come back and visit them.

At that time, I did not know what the purpose of that pamanhiin was and although it was usually obligatory, my parents disallowed the people from carrying me across the casket. Although Filipinos are known to adhere strictly to their traditions, rituals, and beliefs, my parents raised my siblings and me differently.

As infants, my siblings and I were not baptized in a Catholic church. We grew up in a Fundamental Bible Baptist Christian home that was based on biblical values and principles. The church and school that we attended were established with the influence of U.S. missionaries who came to the Philippines to start Baptist congregations. Our private Christian school taught us both Filipino and American subjects that focused on biblical standards. I recall memorizing scripture verses before each final exam, listening to devotions and singing hymnal songs every morning, and doing many more rituals. It was our family's tradition to attend church services every Sunday, and midweek prayer meeting services every Wednesday. I even visited nearby barangays or small communities to assist with gospel classes and medical mission efforts. Our church has had a great influence on the traditions and practices that my family believes in.

My mother, who was a devoted Christian, helped raise us to be God-fearing and become steadfast Bible believers. With the help of our pastor, she instilled in us the importance of faith and salvation. At our church, it was emphasized that we must live our life based on faith in God, obeying the Bible, and not through the common traditional Filipino beliefs.

I was seven years old, back in 1998, when I learned more about the relation of death and the need for salvation. I remember attending a Baptist Youth Impact for elementary to college age youngsters. Our church had about 500 visitors that evening and I was seated in one of the theatre-styled chairs in the balcony. We watched a screening of the movie Left Behind by Tim Lahaye. This movie was based on a book series that depicts what would happen on the earths' last days. I clearly recall watching a scene from this movie, where a group of passengers aboard a red-eye flight lost their loved ones seated next to them and all that was left was their clothes. Bible believers understand this scene as the "rapture." The rapture is also known as the second coming of Christ when Jesus Christ returns to earth to gather his children and bring them with Him to heaven. Immediately after the movie's end, I remember crying heavily as I was emotionally overwhelmed. I remember thinking that I would not want to be included with the people who would be left behind or suddenly die without knowing where I would end up, either heaven or hell. I was bawling in fear and worry over my relatives who did not know about what is to come and for my relatives who have not yet been saved and might end up in hell.

During the sermon, the pastor preached that all men are bound to die somehow, but through God's grace and by receiving His Son, Jesus Christ into our hearts, we can be saved. These are the only ways to save us from going to hell.

Afterward, the church service held an invitation for individuals who were willing to repent their sins and accept Jesus Christ in their life. I recall humbling myself in front of the crowd and walking in the middle of the aisle while the song Just As I Am was playing. I remember not being able to contain my emotions and kneeling down in front of the altar, praying, crying, and at the same time asking God for forgiveness. I recall my first-grade teacher, Ms. Micu, approaching me and kneeling down with me to pray. She assured me that from that day on, I became a child of God and even if I were to die that day, I was confident that I will be going to heaven. This event has been one of the most treasured, unforgettable, and important moments in my life.

Being raised in a Christian environment helped me appreciate the heart and the desire of the American missionaries that came to the Philippines to minister to the Filipino people, witness for the people salvation, and share the word of God. As a family, we learned to believe in the power of prayer in times of happiness, in times of contentment, in times of sickness, in times of struggles, in times of sorrow, and in times of grief. We learned to keep the faith in everything that we encounter and everything that we do.

We also learned not to be sorrowful at the loss of a loved one but rather appreciate the time that was granted to us with the person. During my aunt's funeral service, we made sure that we sang hymnal songs that reflected her life. My middle sister and I sang a duet entitled, All Because of God's Amazing Grace, which chronicles the assurance that death is not the end but rather a new beginning of life.

My perspective of death has changed ever since I came to know Christ. Although I still fear death and the uncertainty of not knowing when a person will die, I think that I have come to realize that dying is normal and part of our human nature. I believe that my Christian upbringing helps me to have a different, yet a positive, perspective on life and death. As I continue to reflect on the ways that my parents have raised me and my siblings, I will, without a doubt pass on this same type of upbringing I experienced to the next generation. After all, kaligtasan or salvation is one of the greatest gifts a person can ever receive in one's life and it happens because of God's amazing grace.

Jeramae wrote this as a fourth year nursing student at Chaminade University of Honolulu. She moved to Hawai'i when she was 10 and can proudly say that she is still verbally fluent in Tagalog. She believes "When I think of my Savior alone on the cross, know without Him that my life would be lost. If He had not been willing to suffer the cost, to rescue a sinner like me."

Twenty
I DIDN'T KNOW WHAT I DIDN'T KNOW
by Inda Manuel Gage

"A journey is only truly complete when you return to where it began." This airline advertisement on board Cathay Pacific attracted my attention, as it pertains to my present journey. The 16-hour non-stop flight from JFK to Hong Kong and another two hours to Manila allowed me to reflect on my life. John, my husband and traveling companion of 44 years, and I are on our way to Bacolod City for my 50th high school reunion at St. Scholastica's Academy in Bacolod where it all started—my life in a suitcase, my lifetime of travels!

I didn't know what I didn't know…that there was a vast world of wonder and excitement out there waiting for me to explore. In 1964, barely 16 years old, I was told by my parents that I was going to Australia under the Rotary International Exchange Program. I don't remember being consulted, but I'm sure I got in by default. My older brother had rejected the opportunity. To save face, my parents offered my name as an alternate. Despite the fact that I was a happy sophomore student in my high school and my social circle, there was no arguing, no discussion. The suitcase was packed and off I went on my first trip abroad.

It was a year's journey, an amazing adventure! I stayed with nine families, moving every six weeks all around the city of Adelaide, the capital of South Australia. Going to school was a challenge. The means of transport and route changed every six weeks. I went by bus, tram, train, or if I got lucky, I got driven by car. Luckily, St. Aloysius College was in the center of the

...n all-girls convent school very much like my school in Bacolod.

Now, how were the nine families different? Very much so! The very first family I stayed with were gourmands and wine connoisseurs, an older couple whose children were adult professionals. The evenings started with cocktails, followed by three kinds of wines matching the three-course dinner. To say the least, it was quite a stretch for me, whose choices back home were water and soda which we Ilongos called "Coks." Homework became a mighty task after three or four drinks, so I did them at dawn, when the buzz would clear off my head. This was only beginner's luck, as meals deteriorated quickly after I moved to the next family. I had my share of pork 'n beans on toast for breakfast and marmite sandwiches for lunch, healthy but tasted like motor oil to me. When I stayed with Catholic families, Friday nights meant fish and chips wrapped in newspaper, bought at a neighborhood store, eaten sitting on the sidewalks with my foster siblings. Cool! All taboo in my Pinoy upbringing—with unwashed ink-blotted hands eating greasy foods, sitting on dirty ground. I could feel my mother cringing at this scenario. Was this a start of my liberation—dirt can be so much fun! I was also a very slow eater, brought up to be mahinhin (demure and ladylike). I struggled through my meals; dagger-eyed siblings watching me chew my food, impatiently waiting for dessert, which can't be served until this slow poke is done eating.

Best treat of my life was my introduction to the arts and culture. My host Rotary Club got me a month's subscription to the events of the Royal Festival of Arts, an annual event in Adelaide. World renowned singers, actors, musicians, and dancers—all top of the line! For starters, the Queen of England, HRH Queen Elizabeth, came for a visit. What a thrill waving to royalty as the Queen paraded the streets. A week or so later, on these same streets, mass hysteria hit! The Fab Four—John, Paul, George and Ringo—the Beatles were in town! Lucky me, I was given a ticket by my Rotarian counselor to watch the

Beatles concert. Mahinhin went out the window. Of course, I screamed my head off, but I didn't faint like the other girls did. I was glad to be a part of a true phenomenon.

More high culture at this Festival, I got to see Margot Fonteyn of the Royal Ballet; a Shakespearean play performed in the Globe Theater Tent; Andres Segovia, a famous Spanish classical guitarist; Diana Ross and the Supremes. I didn't know then that 20 years later, I would live in the next town to Diana in Connecticut. We shared a Polish carpenter who would drop me when Ms. Ross called. To my surprise, among this impressive roster of talents, the Philippines was represented by the Bayanihan Philippine Folk Dance Co. My entire school went to watch their matinee show, my first time to see them perform. Yes, I was aware that they were world famous, but like everyone else I was in awe with the show. They showcased the diversity of cultures of the Philippines in dance with such bravura, precision, and excitement that I was mesmerized. In fact, I was smitten! I thought to myself, I will join this company when I grow up. Do I dare dream?

The year in Australia was a big learning curve for a 16 year old. I had experienced a different culture other than my own and I had shared my own culture with Australia. From this experience, I knew that I am a Filipina and proud of it.

I also knew that I had caught the travel bug. My world had opened up! I came home to Bacolod with pasalubong (gifts) for the family, stories to tell in my acquired Aussie twang, which was short-lived as the Ilongo singsong accent came right back. Back at St. Scholastica for my senior year, I graduated from high school in 1966.

Australia was the start of my lifetime of travels. We are now in the year 2016. Where did the last 50 years take me?

College was in Manila. Bayanihan was still foremost in my mind, only to find out that one had to be enrolled at Philippine Women's University where the dance company is affiliated. This regulation isn't true today. To my horror and

175

disappointment, my strict father put his foot down. "You are not enrolling at PWU." My dream was crushed! Back to the nuns.

So, off to St. Paul's College I enrolled. I tried the Glee Club that first year but found myself dancing the next year with the Paulinian Dance Troupe. Our trainer was a former Bayanihan dancer, who arranged for Bayanihan male dancers to partner with us for our year-end recital. What a twist of fate! Three of us from our school were picked to train and audition with Bayanihan. We passed! It was written in my stars! I danced with Bayanihan without my father knowing it. Performances in the beginning were limited to Saturday afternoon recitals at PWU for tourists. Stage make-up and false eyelashes were removed before I got home.

But when I started to perform late nights and had passed the audition for a Japan trip, I knew I couldn't hide the truth any longer from my father. My mother was in cahoots with me the entire time. My father sensed he couldn't hold me back any longer, so he gave me his blessing. I then enrolled at PWU so I could join in performances and tours abroad. Days were spent juggling between my college courses and hours and hours of dance rehearsals. To make it to any tour abroad, we had to go thru a series of auditions.

That first year, I traveled with the company to Japan, Australia, and New Zealand. The big tour coming up was the International Tour of 1970-71 with 13 months of world travel. Highly competitive, over 300 dancers auditioned for 36 spots.

Aside from the dance ability, and audition criteria included the "Bayanihan smile," the blending of faces on stage so no one's look sticks out, and passing psychological tests to make sure the dancers can take the pressure and rigors of travel and performing. With hard work and lots of prayers, I earned a spot in this International Tour, the culmination of my Bayanihan career.

Inda and Ramon Obusan performed the "Banga" and the Kalinga wedding dance for the Bayanihan Dance Company.

traveled through three continents, 20 countries and ., performing eight or more times a week for 56 weeks. We performed for culture lovers throughout the world and for royalty like King Olaf of Oslo, Queen Margarethe of Denmark, Prime Minister George Pompidou of France, and other dignitaries. Highlights of our tour included performing for the Ed Sullivan Show, (the Beatles performed two years before us), in the ruins of the Temple of Baalbeck in Lebanon to Beirut's elite, as well as the USSR as the cultural exchange mission with the Bolshoi Ballet when Russia was still closed to world travel.

Life on the road with a company of 42 (including staff members) was fun but physically tiring and emotionally draining. We laughed, we cried, we loved, we fought—we became a family—for life. The dance company was appropriately named Bayanihan. The word "bayanihan" means to work together as in building the bahay kubo (the nipa hut found in the rural regions). This best describes our collective effort to put up a good energized show, night after night. Tough to keep the show fresh, we played tricks on stage to keep the joy flowing. Tito Lardie, our artistic director would remind us to put kislap (sparkle) in our eyes before going on stage. It was always a satisfying and exhilarating feeling when we got to curtain call, as we bowed with gratitude to thunderous applause from the audience. Job well done, company! Followed by our chuckles, "Nakaloko na naman tayo" (we fooled them again). As the stage lights went down so did our spirits, as we left the stage, giving way to exhaustion, moods, loneliness, homesickness, and HUNGER!

In the eyes of the beholder, our lives couldn't be anything but charm and glam! Often times, we were treated to champagne and caviar receptions with royalty and dignitaries which tickled our fancies for the moment. Charming in our barongs and balintawak (Filipiniana gowns), armed with our "Bayanihan smiles," we giggled to each other our little secret— that underneath our beautiful embroidered calado outfits were our stinky dried-up sweats and grimy dirty feet from our last show. If only they knew! There were times when all we wanted was to relish a quiet private moment in our hotel rooms to enjoy our adobo or sinigang and rice after the show. For a buck a meal, these much-missed Pinoy comfort foods were prepared by some entrepreneurial chefs in the group, feeding our bodies and nourishing our souls. No hamburgers nor hot dogs can fuel our energies and spirits to fork out Pinoy culture to our audiences. Bring on the tuyo (dried fish)!

Bayanihan and most especially our choreographer, Lucrecia Urtula, whom we fondly called Mommy Urts, gave me a most valuable gift, my self confidence! Before the auditions for the International Tour, Mommy assigned me a flirtatious dance, "Cumbia" from South America, for a special show of international dances. I cried and pleaded, "I couldn't possibly project that dance as I don't have it in me to be flirtatious." I was the mahinhin, raised to be a dalagang Filipina. Can't argue with Mommy, I had to dance it. I didn't know what I didn't know then, that she was eyeing me for a solo dance in the next international tour for another sexy and flirtatious dance, the "Banga" (the Kalinga Pot Dance). She was able to see and pull out something that I thought was beyond me. If pigs can fly, I guess, so can I! Thank you, Mommy. I was happy to be selected to dance the Banga, partnered by Ramon Obusan (who later formed his own dance company and was awarded the National Artist for Dance. Mommy Urtula got the same award in another year). I was part of the research team led by Ramon who traveled to Kalinga for two weeks and lived with the Kalinga tribe. We observed their way of life, recorded it, came back to Manila and worked on creating their culture to dance form. Thus evolved Banga and the Kalinga Wedding Dance as part of our Northern repertoire for the International Tour. This experience is so invaluable to me. I felt I was a true Kalinga as I performed the dance on stage.

An absolute dream come true! Traveling the different countries, experiencing their cultures and their arts were highly fulfilling and enriching for me and so were the joys and rigors of performing. Did we have fun? Yes, and that is an understatement! Yet, somehow I felt I came home from military duty, disciplined, responsible, confident, and committed. I lived the fact that "the show must go on," no matter what. Unless we really couldn't hold our heads up due to illness, we were on that stage dancing our hearts out, giving it our all. What was ingrained in us was that each and everyone was an integral part of a whole. We were an ensemble working together to deliver professionalism in our commitment to the mission we signed up for. We were Ambassadors of Goodwill for the Philippines in Dance. Medals for the "war heroes"? My father was proud of me! It was something I fought for.

In 1972, back in Manila, there I was resting my tired feet from all the dancing, I found myself quietly reminiscing on my travels and contemplating what to do next. Along came this tall, handsome guy with sexy sideburns. I didn't know what I didn't know then, that this was my knight in shining armor, made in America. It started with a blind date arranged by a very dear friend. She hasn't met him yet but purely from intuition, she guessed that John Gage was the right guy for me. The courtship went fast, as John took risks of being swallowed up by open manholes, wading through the chronic Manila floods when he came to pick me up for our dates. Another Bayanihan International Tour for 1973 was tempting me to sign up again for more travels, but instead I signed a marriage contract on August 19, 1972. We got married on Villa Ramona Beach in Ormoc, Leyte where my family had relocated. John was working for Pepsi International from the New York office. John's parents came to our wedding from Rockford, Illinois, a town north of Chicago that had one Chinese restaurant where my in-laws had chicken chow mein, maybe once. That was about the extent of their taste of the exotic. Influenced by my Bayanihan background, the theme of the wedding was Filipiniana. A jusi (local fiber) calado gown and barong was fashioned within 24-hours for my in-laws. My simple jusi gown was coutured by a friend I met in Paris, Larry Silva, who was working at the House of Pierre Balmain in Paris. He happened to be in Manila at that time. As the sun was setting, we exchanged our marriage vows (including the vow to travel. Ha! Ha!). A wedding on the beach at sunset time, 400 guests and seven lechons (roasted pigs)! Do you think that was exotic enough for my in-laws? They talked about it for a long time.

Seven months after the wedding, John took a two-year job assignment with Pepsi in Toronto, Canada. Then it was time to settle down—a new job for John at Chase Manhattan Bank in NYC, a house in Stamford, Connecticut, commuting distance to NYC. We bought a "money-pit," an old Mediterranean built in 1920, which we spent years renovating. In this home we raised our three children: Malen, Sean, and Marla. Believe it or not, we still are in residence there since 1975. Both John and I love our close proximity to NYC where we can enjoy the best in the arts and culture, reminiscent of my Festival of Arts experience in Adelaide half a century ago.

So, what happened to this world traveler? John was offered an assignment to the Netherlands in 1986. Guess what? I didn't want to go. I was deeply rooted in Connecticut with mothering our kids who were too young to travel. However, I didn't have a choice. The job is where the money is. So, for six years, 1986-1992, we left Connecticut. We lived in the Netherlands for two years and in the U.K. for four years. My travel bug was re-awakened and it bit my kids too. With three young kids in tow, we meandered through many countries in Europe, Greece, Turkey, and traveled within England and Holland. It was at this time that I got more exposed to European arts and in fact I took a year diploma course at Victoria and Albert Museum in London. Living and traveling in Europe developed my "third eye!"

We had occasional trips to the Philippines as it was important for our kids to know my Philippine culture and their heritage. These trips were mostly timed for my Mom's birthday since she loved to have big celebrations for her special day.

, our family In the U.S. had big parties for special days of food and a gathering of friends with a program of songs and dances. During the summer of 1996, we decided to do a "Philippine culture immersion" vacation. For two months, the three kids and I traveled to the place where I was born, where I grew up, where I went to school, where I spent my summer vacations, etc. They got to meet practically everyone that had touched my life growing up: Relatives, household helpers, my classmates and friends, my Bayanihan family.

We also traveled to many touristic spots, as far north as Banaue and Sagada, and as far south as Davao and Zamboanga. It was on these trips that I collected Philippine paintings, folk arts, and some furniture, which I hauled home by air cargo. There is no mistaking that a Filipina lives at our home by its décor. For someone who never cooked before I got married, I express my being a Filipino mostly through my cooking of Filipino food. At our church fairs, I started a booth selling Filipino lunch plates, introducing Filipino cuisine to our church community. My kids grew up loving adobo, pancit, lumpia, torta, empanada. When our kids eventually left home, my "pabaon" to each one was a bottle of Rufina Patis and Silver Swan soy sauce for their own kitchens. They surely have acquired the joy of food and the importance of gathering of family and friends, which I attribute to being Filipino. Our kids felt that growing up with both the Filipino and American cultures is a definite plus.

The years went by so quickly that we find ourselves now enjoying our three grandkids. Our granddaughter Leilani is five years old, blond and blue-eyed which makes me look like the Pinay nanny when we are together. The younger brother whose name is Gage is three and has more of an olive complexion, a hint of the Pinoy blood! Our new addition is Baby Johnny; it's too early to tell if there is any trace of Pinoy in him at all. It has become a tradition that I cook pancit for long life for the grandkids' birthdays. This assures me that my Filipino food carries through to the next generation.

When John retired from work in 2003, we chose Hawai'i to be our second home. Since his first visit to Oahu in 1972, on his way to the Philippines, he had this dream of coming to Hawai'i and be a beach bum. I don't really know what he meant by that. Swimming, surfing? Oh no! One hardly finds us on the beach, except on early morning walks and on our beach chairs at nightfall, meditating on the glorious sunsets. Typical Filipina, I hide from the sun during the day. It must be the notion of "doing nothing" that brings us to Hawai'i twice a year. But there are still more countries to visit in our bucket list.

Going back to where I started, "A journey is only complete when you return to where it began." Finally, we arrived in Bacolod City for my 50th high school reunion. I came back to St. Scholastica, the school that gave me a solid foundation for my life. I came in a spirit of sincere gratitude to the German Benedictine nuns who taught me: "To thine own self be true," words by Shakespeare, words I lived by these past 50 years. My teachers are long gone now. I wanted them to see me, "the impertinent girl" as they called me, who was not allowed inside the classroom because I asked too many questions. My desk was moved in the hallway for Theology class. I have not changed much in that aspect, I still am a seeker! I know in my heart that all they wanted for me was to have a good life, a happy one. I am here to report that I have that, I am that! And I thank them ever soooo much!

We had a very small class of 28. I kept in touch with most of my classmates over the years by coming to Bacolod for class reunions or I see them when they come to visit the East Coast. I have no family left in Bacolod but I always believed that I can come home to Bacolod when I am ready. Can I really? Will Bacolod embrace this long-gone daughter? I wonder! After several days of seeing everyone and enjoying all the activities, I became introspective. I sensed a difference in attitudes with my classmates. Did they change? Did I change? Was I too forward in expressing my views? Did they agree with my views? Did I offend someone for giving my opinion even if they asked it? Can I be myself with this crowd? WHO AM I?

I guess I am this Filipina who had traveled early and traveled far; learned my life lessons from my travels; loves and respects the arts and cultures of the world because they feed my soul; believes in the universality of all religions; loves my family and friends; loves to dance (disco and folk); does yoga and gardening; expresses my Filipino culture through home décor and cooking.

I am eternally grateful for all my blessings! My experiences over those 50 years of living in different places, learning different life styles, interacting and making new friends from different cultures have helped to shape me the way I have become. But I remain a Filipina at heart.

Hardly anyone mistakes me for someone other than a Filipina, but I have ideas and responses that do not always reflect a typical Filipina to most. Perhaps, I symbolize an aspect of diversity among Filipinas by having a different outlook on life about some things and it's all right to be different as long as one is comfortable in one's skin. I am. This I feel is my legacy to my children, that they feel comfortable in their own skins no matter what. And my biggest hope is that they keep an open mind and never give up on exploring the wonders of this world!

My travels started in Bacolod. When I left in 1964, I didn't know what I didn't know. Now that I returned, does my journey end here? No, because there is still a big wide world to explore and while I will never know all there is to be known, I do know that there is still a lot for me to know. I didn't know what I didn't know!

Inda Manuel Gage lives in Stamford, Connecticut with her husband John and considers Hawai'i as their second home. They love to travel to experience the arts and culture of other countries. Inda loves to garden, dance, and do yoga.

184

Twenty One
CULTURE BEARER OF THE FILIPINO DIASPORA
by Pepi Nieva

No, I didn't plan to write. I've been too immersed in trying to live in the moment, like the self-help books say you should, so that I've been forgetting about the past. Until I heard the first stories for this anthology read in a library room at University of Hawai'i at Manoa.

That's me! I realized. A self-identified, dyed-in-sinamay culture bearer of the Filipino diaspora! Even though when I first started culture bearing, I didn't even know there was a diaspora. At that time, OFW was not yet in the common lexicon and I didn't leave my homeland looking for a better life. My life in Manila was fine, thank you.

Right after college, I was living in relative freedom compared to my chaperoned, convent-school days. After all, I was past 21 and my parents were too busy with their own lives—co-founders of the Christian Family Movement; active in the opposition against martial law; members of the Citizen's Council for Mass Media, etc.—to keep a close eye on their three adult daughters, one of whom was discovering her country and lots of other things as well.

I was then working at the Philippine Department of Tourism and as a magazine writer and was finding a world of wonder that planted many a culture-bearing seed: A four-day wedding in Lanao for a Maranao princess whose dowry included carabaos, coconuts, and cavans of rice (see how women are prized in our country!); fuchsia, green, and golden rice, pounded into paper-thin leaves, hanging below capiz shell

during Lucena's pahiyas harvest festival; bango clay
ɔnting patis and bagoong; and Ilocos fishermen eating
fish raw, straight from the nets.

My prized possessions included a boar's tusk necklace
from my favorite Baguio market, a brass, three-inch bracelet
from Marawi worn with batik malong, wooden ganta (rice
measuring container), and a baul (chest) decorated with inlaid
carabao horn from Mindanao via an Ermita antique shop.

In those carefree, pre-children days, we climbed an ashy
volcano, rode buses with chickens hanging out of open sides,
and camped in secluded beaches with only a fisherman's hut for
shelter and the cogon grass for a toilet. My parents rarely
questioned whether I was really sleeping over at a friend's house
instead of somewhere else far more exciting. Of course I still
lived at home and was driven to and from work by the family
chauffeur.

Later, I learned to drive, in Manila traffic, no less. The
little green car was all my new husband (but old boyfriend) and
I could afford on a writer's (mine) and TV/radio personality
(his) salaries. When Emil (Charlie Brown for DZRJ rock radio
fans) and I got married, I kept my name. Manila's media and
arts culture was steeped in the freer, semi-hippie ethos of the
times. But it was also the martial law era when dissenters
disappeared and jailed family friends escaped in secret to
become refugees in other countries. Companies were
sequestered by the Marcos regime, including my husband's
radio station, which was being supervised, albeit benignly, by an
army colonel. So when Emil was asked by the station owner,
Ramon Jacinto, to join him in Hawai'i where his family was in
exile—the martial law government had taken over Jacinto Steel
and all Jacinto companies—we said yes.

But we were not escaping to the U.S. To us, it was
another adventure.

So I was not prepared for the culture shock presented by
1970s Hawai'i.

Pepi and second son Nicolo Quinto dressed in Mindanao batik malong (his) and embroidered kimona (hers) at the Pasko! Christmas celebration at the Honolulu Museum of Arts. Nicolo is now a U.S. Army officer.

Aside from abysmal ignorance about washing machines and vacuum cleaners, preparing meals, and shutting cabinet doors, let alone taking care of a baby (the help did all that in Manila), I was shocked that:

People were shocked that I spoke good English.

My rigorous Philippine education and work experience did not count for much in the eyes of potential employers.

Some Filipinos were ashamed to admit they were Filipino!

It was obvious. I had to become Pinay: Culture Bearer of Hawai'i Filipinos.

I felt that sharing Filipino culture and tradition in its rich depth and diversity would be the best way to instill pride. I wanted to inoculate my children from prejudice by arming them with history, infusing them with knowledge, and exposing them to their mother country's treasure trove of artifacts, arts, and crafts. I told them our family's stories so that they would know who they are and where they came from.

They would not be harmed when some uninformed person threw around derogatory descriptions of Filipinos, like bukbuk (termites) or poke-knife. They would never be told, like some students, that Filipinos were meant for service jobs and not college. When asked, they would be able to share how Datu Lapulapu defeated the explorer Magellan in Mactan island off Cebu; the romance hidden behind folk tales about mystic mountains and bamboos birthing the first couple Malakas and Maganda; and why renaissance men and revolutionary heroes chose to fight for our mother country's freedom from colonial rule.

So I read them books imported from the Philippines. A favorite was about the magic jeepney that whisked you to faraway places and made wishes come true. I brought them to events showcasing Filipino music, dance, games, and traditions. My oldest son, who bore the brunt of my indoctrination, remembers the trips we managed to make to the Philippines, and the Filipino summer school ran by Operation Manong when he reluctantly learned to say "magandang gabi" (good night) and dance the maglalatik, the coconut dance.

I kept my old magazines featuring Filipino history and life as research resources. I soaked up many new things, too, about Hawai'i and its Filipinos as we joined several Filipino organizations. When I was writing, editing, and managing the *Hawai'i Filipino News*, I delved into the trials and triumphs of the sakada and plantation life, narratives that were not part of our curriculum in the Philippines. It was also a revelation to see for the first time the money dance at emceed weddings, and to learn that eskrima/arnis de mano martial arts were alive and thriving in Hawai'i. These also were not part of my Manila experience.

Unfortunately, my kids never learned to speak Tagalog, except for a few words like naman, bahala na, and some bodily functions that I think the grandkids also know. I blame that on 1) my colonial upbringing in which the nuns fined us for speaking the native language, and 2) my husband's broken Taglish. Not his fault. He grew up in the "States."

We were lucky in that, missing our relatives back home, we were able to cobble together an extended family of friends first found through school mates who had moved to Hawai'i, including one of the founders of the then newly formed Oahu Filipino Jaycees. We expanded our Jaycee group to include sisters and brothers-in-law, the kumare of one of my aunts in Manila, and more newly arrived classmates and friends. For the past 40 years, we have been spending holidays and birthdays together. When the kids were young, we would all squeeze, Filipino-style, into vacation homes and condos and play mahjong, along with tennis. When typhoons hit the Philippines, we caroled at people's houses to raise money. Without the support of our adopted family, I wouldn't have survived when my marriage broke up.

This family is what my second son mentions when asked

about his "Filipino upbringing." He also remembers the Pasko! celebrations presented by our organization, the Filipino Association of University Women, and the Filipino Christmas carols I used to play while decorating the advent wreath and the tree each December.

By the time he was growing up in the 1990s, attitudes towards Filipinos in Hawai'i had progressed, perhaps because, now in its fourth generation, Filipinos were becoming more integrated into the local culture. Although the largest number of newcomers to Hawai'i continued to be (and still are) Filipinos, Micronesians and other Pacific Islanders were now the newest group on Hawai'i's ethnic block. Earlier, when I was working with the Filipino paper, we were still counting firsts: First Filipino university graduate; first doctor; first dentist, and so on. By the 1990s, there were too many achievers to count. Foremost among them was Ben Cayetano, whose election as the first (!) governor of Filipino ancestry in Hawai'i signaled to many that we had arrived on the political and social map.

But all these had not erased the old stereotypes of dog eating and knife poking, said second son. He was sometimes teased and at least on one occasion, barred from the family table of an immigrant Chinese family who looked askance at Filipinos. Then there was the day in grade school when he announced he wanted to be Japanese. "All my friends were Japanese so I wanted to conform and be like everyone else. Japanese culture is very strong in Hawai'i and at that time a lot of the popular influences come from there," he explains now.

I was appalled! Didn't my culture-bearing mission have any effect at all? Was it merely a pathetic coaching attempt that went in one ear and out the other?

I decided to ask my sons, "How did you feel about your exposure to Filipino culture and tradition? Does being Filipino matter?"

At first pass, the answer appears to be no.

Eldest son says growing up with Filipino culture didn't

make any difference one way or the other. On the other hand, this very local boy never felt ashamed of being Filipino (inoculated?). It's even cool to be Filipino now, he reports, citing the up-and-coming food scene and the success of entertainers like hip-hop dancers belonging to Vegas headliner Jabbawockeez and part-Filipino stars like singer Pharell Williams. His two kids take for granted that they're Filipino, but first grandchild is taking Chinese, not Tagalog, courtesy of his Chinese popo (grandmother) and Japanese gigi (grandfather).

Second son says he identifies first as an American "especially due to my military service where I've had to serve as a cultural ambassador representing my country oversees," and second, as an Asian Pacific Islander. For a six-month language course, he decided to learn Russian to add to his Chinese, instead of Tagalog. Since he can't speak Tagalog, he feels unqualified to share Filipino-ness with any children he will have in the future and besides, he would have to consult his future wife on their upbringing.

And yet, in his search for identity, he has sought out his father's relatives in California and dug deep into army records for the accomplishments of both grandfathers during World War II. On a recent trip to Manila, he discovered the strong and enduring pull of the Filipino family. "Despite the distance and low level of contact over the years, the familial connection is so strong that it transcends anything else I've experienced," he says. As for his shopping priorities? A piña barong and a capiz parol were his big ticket expenditures.

Filipinos and part-Filipinos comprise 25 percent of Hawai'i's population and growing. But frictions between local and immigrant remain and groups like Farrington High School's F.O.B. project are still addressing pride and shame and the Filipino identity. So I continue my self-appointed mission through FAUW projects like this one. Whenever slivers of opportunity arise, I don't hesitate to expound on Philippine values, traits, culture and the arts, and ancestral histories.

"Sometimes I do listen to you, Mom," second son says. There's always hope for us culture bearers.

 *Pepi Nieva is a writer, editor, and public relations professional who has worked with corporate, government, agency, media, and non-profit institutions and served in various boards and organizations in Hawai'i. She now lives in Honolulu and in Oregon with her husband, John M. Brown, but has left a substantial part of her heart in the Philippines.*

NEXT GENERATION

Young model at fashion show during FAUW's Pasko! celebration

Twenty Two
FILIPINOS VS. FOBS
by Kristen Labiano

I *hate* Evelyn Dela Cruz. She's so FOB!

...What does "FOB" mean?
And what do you mean you hate her? She's so nice!

What? You don't know? Fresh Off the Boat.
She says things like
"Can you help me *por* improobing my pehper *por* de homewark?"
Ha! Stupid FOB.
Like...what the *fuck* are you even *saying?*
If you can't speak propertively, like why even bother trying?
And she *smells* like patis. Ugh!
She's just *so* Filipino. It's *so* gross.
That's why I hate her.

...Yea but...*we're* Filipino, too.

Well...yea, but I'm not **FOB**. I don't speak with that stupid FOB-by accent.
I was *born* Americanized.
I speak in a way so people can actually *understand* what the hell I'm saying.
I can actually pronounce my F's.

Well that's because she comes from someplace else.
English is her second language, not her first.
Geeze...

What is it about Evelyn that you **hate** *so much*?

She's so LOUD and she laughs like *all* the time.
And I heard that she's a real *slut*.

How do you even <u>know</u> this?

Jacquelyn told me.

Didn't Jacquelyn sleep with your ex?
Yea?

Isn't that why you broke up with him?

…She's a slut, too. That's why she'd know.

…She's never even had a boyfriend before
And I like Evelyn, though.
At her birthday party last week, she let me try some of her
mom's
adobo at her house.
So good!
And when I brought my mom's lumpia
she asked me for the recipe.
And when we were watching "Maria Clara"
Evelyn was translating the words for me
from Tagalog to English
so I could follow along better.

I wouldn't trust her, though.
Like I said, she's a FOB.
She's not like us.
We're not the same.

So…you don't like adobo and lumpia with vinegar?
…I do…

And don't you watch those soap operas on
TFC with your mom every night, at dinner too?

195

…Yea I do
…but that's different.
She's just so…so…I don't know, she's just a FOB.
And her voice is so irking.
You can't even understand what she's saying.
Mind as well not even try.
And like I said. She's slutty.
A dirty, patis-smelling, non-virgin skanky FOB slut.
I told you.
We're not the same.

Yea…you're right.
You and Evelyn **aren't** the same.

MY FATHER'S SOFTNESS

Taking a break from studying, I make my way into the kitchen
I find my father barefoot, as usual,
standing next the stove in his worn out, faded
red tank top and khaki cargo shorts.
"What's for dinner, Dad?" I ask. His eyes stay fixated on the pan
before him
"My adobo!" he announces.
His voice a melodic warmth
that dances towards the sky from his grin
as he stirs the carne baboy with a large wooden spoon.
They cheer as I hover over them,
inhaling the salty scent with a smile.
"Mmmm," I say.
I look at him, his brow furrowed in concentration
yet lined with a hint of that smile
The smoke envelopes his face
with nothing but the sound of sizzling pork surrounding us
I watch him in comforting quiet
as I do every day, in near silence.
Father never does say much. But I still hear him.

It is in his softness where he speaks the most.

When he talks in Ilokano,
telling my brother and I
to wash our dishes and sweep our floor.
Never forget where you come from.

As he washes our clothes
and hangs them up to dry
one
by
one
Stay warm and healthy, my children.

When he carries those heavy boxes of perishables
from the airline caterer to his transport truck and
into the airplane
at hours on end.
In the cold and heat.
You will not be hungry.

When he thought I was in deep sleep
walking into my bedroom
placing a tender kiss on my forehead
as he would leave for another day
of "heart" work at 3 a.m.
I love you.

 *Kristen Labiano is a proud arts enthusiast and enjoys creating, performing, as well as observing an eclectic array of the matter. With a degree in Humanities, concentration English, she hopes to continue to dabble in the arts through writing, music, and/or theatre. This will be her first official published work and she hopes that there will be more to come in the future.*

Twenty Three
A FULL-TIME MOTHER
by Faith Pascua

At night in my house, when everyone should be sleeping, eyes closed, minds drifting towards wonderland, she's still awake in the living room flipping through memories of what used to be.

She's crying, wishing her storied scrapbook past was reality again.

She reminisces over pages of smiles, compiled accomplishments enough to fill miles of trophy cases. She is the original dust-buster dirt-devil housekeeper winner of the 2006 Housekeeper of the Year award.

She remembers wanting to vacuum the red carpet something majestic.

Floors so shiny, you could see your inner child in the reflection. She idolizes perfection.

That hotel was her home away from home, her fortress of solitude and it has been for over 16 years. She cleans hotel rooms, finds the history in dirty laundry, closet skeletons, and linens. Knows what happens in honeymoon suites, and capable to clean the fuck out of it.

She knows that business trips are filled with more personal endeavors anyway, seeing infidelity with the mistake of forgetting the "do not disturb" sign on the doorknob.

She has seen it all…

Until last fall, when my brother and I watched her crumble under the fall of the economy. The uncertainty placed her waiting by the phone.

She's on call for work now. Today she's number four but they didn't even make it to three.

This job is her first baby, 16 years in the making, not having the experience quite yet. New to baby bottles and cleaning products, at first this job was just to pay the bills, just for now, just until...

It became her passion, found sanctuary in her pink-flowered uniform, and comfort- gelled shoes. She's my mother, sobbing solo under the single light in the living room, resisting to open her scrapbook, trying not to find a reason to be angry at the super natural because she's losing faith. Like a flickering candle...

When she thinks no one is around she still tries her uniform on, this is her battle suit. Her idle hands turn to iron and from wonder woman to wondering woman she feels like she lost her super powers.

My mother is an aglet; found at the tip of shoe laces, she's capable of keeping your sole in place. She will tell you she loves you by just being there...but she's forgotten. Her paycheck is the only way she remembers her value, that coming home without one renders her useless.

Mommy, you are not an ATM, not an automated teller machine.

Worth is not measured in money, your amount balance will never be zero to me.

See, no one remembers what an aglet is. No one cares about the life of the housekeeper who cleaned their hotel room. But mom, you are more than a source of income. You are my monster in the closet inspector, and the detector of sorrow and sobbing anywhere.

Just know when the shake of the money problem earthquake leaves our home, I want you to know I love you more than as a laid off, full-time housekeeper, but as my full-

199

time mother.

This was Faith Angelica Pascua's winning entry in the 2014 Letter to my Parents Contest in Hawai'i, one of the projects sponsored by the FAUW. A graduate of Farrington High School, Faith has won several awards as a performer of slam poetry and has participated in Brave New Voices in Los Angeles representing Youth Speaks Hawai'i.

Twenty Four
EATING CONTEST!
PAPA'S HIDDEN SECRET
by Crystal-Gale M. Sonson

"Family time is making time; for no matter what happens in your life, being with family is worth every second."

My Mom is the oldest child of my Mama and Papa and lucky me was chosen to be the heaven-sent grandchild number one! Praise God right?! But, this also meant that I was destined to be the ideal, responsible role model "manang" for future siblings and cousins. Years have passed and now, Mama and Papa have fourteen grandchildren (seven girls and seven boys) but I never stopped playing role model and baby sitter.

Growing up was a challenge considering that I was the first for well...everything: The first to walk; the first to have a boyfriend; the first to graduate high school; the first college graduate. You get the picture. Yup, there were many "firsts" throughout my life but what many of my cousins may not realize is that I was also "the first" to hear these words from my Papa: "Eating contest!"

"Eating contest!" is what Papa would say to us when it was time to eat dinner. The adults would prepare and set up the dinner table while we, the cousins, would be playing around in the living room until we were called to come to the table. Once we were called, my cousins and I would gather around as the adults (and myself) helped the little ones grab their food. The T.V. would be turned off and all flip phones, toys, and Gameboys were put away. We each sat around the table with my Papa always sitting at the head of the table.

Dinner usually consisted of rice, fish, and some sort of Filipino soup that Mama would make. Chicken papaya is my favorite. Once we all got settled, my Papa would say "Eating contest!" The boys would challenge my Papa in how they can eat more rice than he can while the girls, despite the boys' disgusting faces as they quickly shoved rice in their mouths using their spoons or hands, joined in on the fun. To win, you would have to finish your plate completely with no speck of rice left! Now you would think that this game would stop there, but it didn't. It continued as someone grabbed another scoop of rice or more soup and said that they're on their "second plate" which automatically made them ahead of the others. And then the cycle continued until our stomachs could take no more. Was there ever a real winner you ask? I would say, possibly? But what I can tell you is that we all were determined to win!

This contest continued throughout every family gathering, sleepover, and outing. It was the same routine, no distractions, just a bunch of hungry, determined Filipino kids trying to out-eat each other and their Papa. You can imagine how big and healthy we grew over the years. I would say that the girls had a slight edge of an advantage early on, up until the boys caught up with their growth spurts.

Being the daughter of my grandparents, my Mom too had played this eating game but developed her own way of making sure my brother, sister, and myself would eat all of our dinner: Simply, by force! Just kidding! She would take away our electronics (TV remote, Gameboy, or cellphone) if we didn't want to eat. You know how picky kids can get when it comes to food. Like Papa, Mom would call us to dinner and we would have to put aside all distractions, tie our long hair up into a ponytail to get it out of the way, and sit together as a family. Dad would sometimes eat with us but was often watching ESPN after a long day at work.

Around the summer or fall 2013 the Eating Contest

slowly disappeared. I'm not sure why. This happened at the time I started to attend nursing school. We no longer went over to my grandparents' house as often as we used to although we occasionally got together for the holidays or for family parties. But even then at these parties my Papa never brought up the challenge anymore.

Today, most of us grandchildren are busy with school, extra curricular activities, hanging out with friends, working, or studying. And if we're not doing any of these things, we are found with our phones taking selfies on Snapchatting, scrolling through Instagram, binge watching on Netflix, or like the little ones, playing games on any electronic device we get our hands on. Technology has made it in society.

You can't help but wonder, what's going on? Why haven't I seen my cousins in such a long time? And if I do see them, why aren't we interacting with one another? Have our cell phones been our only way to communicate so that talking to each other face-to-face has become suddenly awkward? Now I have to admit, I too, have been busy. Nursing school is no joke. I learned this the hard way. You're studying from oversized textbooks constantly wherever and whenever, preparing mentally and physically for twelve-hour clinicals, developing poor sleeping habits, and surviving lectures by drinking coffee like there's no tomorrow. However, I regret nothing as it was all worth it.

My family knew that I had to study and they respected that so everyone just let me be as I got into a "study mode" during family gatherings. I'm not sure if I influenced others to bring homework to family parties but I have to admit, I am "the first" to start the habit or practice. Before you know it, all the cousins started to bring their homework. We were all in school, so it made sense, right? We would do our homework together and help each other out. When it was time for dinner we would drop the pencils and gather around the food for the blessing before meals. After we got our plates, rather than sitting with the adults and my Mama and Papa, we would go back into the house or on a separate table to eat our dinner and get right back to studying. This habit of eating dinner separately from the adults started to grow over time. That is, up until I realized what to me was a turning point in understanding the meaning of family.

It was my second semester of nursing school and I was listening to a lecture in a gerontology class. We were having a discussion on grandparents and their role in the family. We each took turns sharing our thoughts and memories, a common thread being that grandparents have many stories and share their words of wisdom from experience amongst their kids and grandkids. I, too, agreed with this but I felt that there was something more, something that captures the true role of grandparents.

I continued to process this thought as I waited for my turn to share. And then, by the grace of God, the memory came to me and I thought about my Papa and how he would always say, "Eating contest!" when my cousins and I were little. I could picture our faces lighting up with excitement and joy as we knew that this contest was one of Papa's favorite things to do with his grandchildren. It was this memory of Papa that made me realize that he wasn't just trying to make sure we eat all of our food to stay healthy, but also to show us the value of family time. That is the true lesson of what Papa was trying to teach his grandchildren. He didn't have to say it directly to us, but rather indirectly expressed his love for us through action and a simple two-word phrase. This moment in gerontology class was no accident. It was a message in disguise to remind me that time with family means everything.

While I drove home from class that day I couldn't help but think of my Mom. Like Papa, family time, eating contest or not, was important for my Mom. Everyday she would come home from work at around four p.m. and would have dinner prepared and ready for us by six p.m. She did this for as long as

I can remember. From when I was a child to now as a young adult, Mom never failed to have dinner on the table for her kids. I know this brief time spent together with was important to her. With studies and work taking most of my time, I was finding it difficult to be on time for dinner. I would either come home late and eat by myself or eat out. I would head to Starbucks or go to the gym to de-stress myself from school, from work, or other problems. This bad habit slowly festered and became what I felt to be an everyday cycle.

A part of me thinks that in the Filipino culture emotions are not verbally expressed but rather shown through action (i.e. working overtime to make sure your children have food on the table or attending your child's sport games to show your support). My Mom today is very open and easy to talk to, but she wasn't always that way. She never questioned or argued about my coming home late. She would simply text me to ask if I planned to be home for dinner. She never once told me, "I want you home for dinner to eat as a family." She simply went about her daily routine to make dinner and go on through the rest of the night. Not once did she express her emotions outwardly in front of my siblings. You can't help but realize that no mother would want to cause concern or pain to her children. I hated being late for dinner because I knew that my Mom enjoys this one meal; out of the entire day she can sit down and spend quality time with her kids. I knew that it was time to stop feeling miserable and disappointed in myself. It was time to take action.

Don't just think about the change, BE THE CHANGE and do something about it. With my Papa's saying "eating contest" as my constant reminder, I sat myself down and, using my planner and time-management skills, I did a self-evaluation of my priorities and necessities. School was important to me and so was getting my foot in the door after graduating from the School of Nursing. But so is family, and family is my everything. It's precious time with family that has helped motivate, support, and encourage me never to give up. It's that

205

quality time and irreplaceable memories of time that I spent with them that have helped me remember why I started.

How easy it is to take for granted the time that we have left to spend with one another because we get caught up with life's demands. After a few adjustments, I was able to find that right amount of balance—to be home for my mother's dinner and later, after helping her clean up and wash dishes, head over to Starbucks to study. I wasn't expecting any outcome from my actions, but I felt the way I did years ago when we sat around the table waiting for my Papa to say: "Eating contest!" Dinner was back, free of distraction, with free time of laughs, jokes, games, and just enjoying one another's company. This time of the day was reserved for family time.

Shortly after this, we had another family gathering at my grandparents' house. You can take a guess about happened when I brought up "Eating contest!" in front of all my cousins. Long story short, let's just say that some things don't change. The younger boys are still learning how to use the Filipino fork-and-spoon technique but have now have developed this slurping sound as they vacuum their plates dry. And yes, the girls still get grossed out by the boys' poor table manners. But aside from the mess on the table, I can see my Papa in his same seat that he always sits in smiling, laughing and telling jokes, surrounded by his grandchildren whom he loves so much. This was one lesson I will never forget, and I thank my Papa for that. No matter how old you get or wherever you may go, there is no better feeling than to find peace and comfort when time is spent together as a family.

Now I didn't tell this story just to talk about my crazy fun Filipino family. What I wanted to share about this story is how making time for family time, as simple as eating a meal together, can impact the lives of the next generations. Time is such a fragile and precious thing that we cannot take back. Growing up as a young teenager, I remember saying how I couldn't wait to get out of the house and be on my own, away from my parents.

What I didn't realize then was that now, after going though college in nursing school and having to work for money, the one thing that I look forward to at the end of the day is to come home and talk face- to-face with people that I love the most, my family. Whether it be a good or a bad day, they are always there to listen, especially during dinner time. I believe that is how we became closer as a family.

In today's generation, social media and preoccupation with self-identity are, sadly, taking the place and time that could otherwise be well spent with others. Too often we see children as young as three who would rather play games on their tablets, iPads, or other electronic devices. It's uncommon to see families at restaurants enjoying the company of one another and having a conversation over dinner without any distractions. Nowadays I see families with their heads bowed, not saying one word to each other, as their faces are glued to their cell phones.

My parents, my Mom in particular, were brought up in the "traditional Filipino ways:" Make sure your kids are in school; make good choices; stay out of trouble, to name a few. They also made sure they knew where we were and what we were doing. Safety was a big concern for my parents but so was education, and they would work long and hard to make sure that my siblings and I would have a bright future ahead of us.

All this, at first, was difficult for me because some my friends didn't understand why I never had a cell phone until I got in middle school when it became necessary to arrange to be picked up. Throughout high school, I hardly ever went out with my friends or went to a sleepover unless my parents knew my friend's parents, and my curfew was 10:00 p.m. I had chores to do every week (dishes, trash, laundry). But what I did have was what I needed: The love of my family.

Although my childhood was difficult because I lived in two cultures at the same time– American and Filipino—I learned to adapt and I continue to be molded and shaped to become the young woman that I am today. My Papa, in particular, was the one who taught me the greatest lesson of all, a lesson we often take for granted—to treasure the value of family time. I plan to continue this tradition and not get so caught up with life's distractions because family is everything. I hope you, too, will find that time with your family. And if you want to add a little fun to it, have an "Eating contest!"

Crystal Sonson is a graduate of Hawai'i Pacific University, Class of 2015. She previously served as HPU's Student Nurses Association president and is the Hawai'i Student Nurses Association co-graduate consultant. She is currently working as a new graduate Pediatric ICU nurse at Kap'iolani Medical Center for Women and Children. In her spare time, she enjoys snorkeling, hiking, and reading at coffee shops.

Twenty Five
TATAY

by Rebecca Carino

Life is strange. We're all busy trying to achieve the grand scheme of our lives, but there are moments when we catch ourselves and think of the ones we love. Just when you miss someone, you actually miss him—sometimes forever.

I had just graduated with a bachelor's degree in English and started my first profession as a learning and success assistant at the University of Hawai'i, West Oahu. I wanted to continue to grow and expand my knowledge, so I applied to graduate school. Many of the school choices I was considering were colleges on the mainland. My mother wept at the thought of her only child going off to the continent with no family to stay with, but she knew it was something I wanted and needed to do. Change was coming, but the change that I experienced was something I hadn't thought about until it actually happened.

January 20, 2016 6:14 p.m.

"Rebecca, where are you?"

"Hi Auntie, I'm at work. Why?"

"Oh thank God, there are police cars and an ambulance outside your grandpa's house."

My heart sunk to my stomach and my insides rearranged themselves in the most unpleasant way. A ball began to form in my throat. All I thought about at that time was my Tatay.

January 20, 2016 6:25 p.m.

"Hey Jonnie, what's going on?"

Rebecca and Tatay.

"I found grandpa lying on the ground. Where are you?"

"I'm at work, is he conscious?"

"I think so."

The ball began to grow to the point where I could not utter any more words, only grunts and sighs. So I hung up and texted: "I'll be there right after work." My eyes started to itch and burn and in reflex I rubbed them only to feel the tears begin to flood down my cheeks. I trembled with each breath and as my coworkers tried to comfort me with semi-emphatic words. I could only hear muffed sounds. I was sinking into the earth. The world I knew was changing, and not in a good way.

My Tatay was a strong and relentless man. I bragged about how, at 84 years old, he was still a sharp as a knife playing Pipito in the back of his red Nissan Frontier while waiting for his grandchildren to finish school. He cheated death many times with cancer and a major heart surgery, but for some odd reason, I believed that his time was up. His strength and vigor played a huge role in my pride of being a Carino.

The next day I rushed to the hospital looking for answers, comfort, familiar faces, but most importantly, hope. There in the room was my Aunt Fely, staring aimlessly into the window murmuring things on her Bluetooth headset. Her eyes instantly lit up when she saw me. I glanced over to see my 5'11" Tatay lying on the bed looking incredibly frail and small. Trying to avoid any more tears, I bombarded my auntie with questions. "Was it a stroke?" "Is he going to get better?" "Why are there tubes in his mouth?"

All the responses were, "I don't know, and neither do the doctors." To see someone as independent and able as my Tatay, only to lie in limbo for an indefinite period of time, was heart wrenching.

Fifteen days! That was all the time that God could spare for us to be with him. My Aunt Fely became the surrogate who made medical decisions on my Tatay's behalf. She then turned to me to come to the hospital and get updates on him so I

211

could share it with the rest of the family. I became the objective voice, explaining the current situation of Tatay to all 11 of his children. But no matter how objective I was or wanted to be, I desperately wanted to cry out for him to be healed and live to see more of what I could accomplish in our family's name.

I remember the last time I spoke to him. I remember how I forgot totally to tell him when my graduation was. He showed up at my graduation lunch with tears in his eyes asking, "Why did you forget about your grandpa?"

I remember how he made the best arroz caldo and dinardaraan and how I would fill my plates up with them, eating till my stomach hurt. Those are two dishes that I will never get to learn to make for him. I remember when he would make my cousins and I line up to kiss him. I could still feel the stubble on his chin and the lingering scent of his cigarette.

February 5, 2016 1:30 a.m.

Phone vibrating.

"Hello?"

"Grandpa just passed away. Come to the hospital now."

At 12:15 a.m., my Tatay left this world. I drove blurry-eyed way above the speed limit to see him; to still see if any earthly essence of his lingered. To kiss and tell him one last time, "Bye Tatay, I love you!" The entire family crowded in and others were milling around outside his room by the time I got there. The heaviness I carried on my way to see him suddenly dissipated. We sat there in warm conversation, and then we began the start of our nine-day prayer.

For the next few days, we would be praying the rosary. Our prayers were offered hoping that Tatay's judgment would be more favorable, that he would be released from purgatory to the gates of heaven. We prayed so that he would not cling to us like Nanay did when we started the nine-day prayer too late. She went into my aunt's body pleading us for help. Atang (offerings) would be given to tatay every time we ate to avoid our food

212

dropping on the floor as that would be a sign that he wanted to eat some. Of course, gambling during these days of mourning, would also take place in honor of him along with hopes of winning money.

One night as we sat around playing cards, a huge brown moth swooped in. It perched itself on one of the pillars in the garage near the light just observing us as we played our hands. There was a moment when the moth fluttered furiously towards my cousin because she was taking too long to play her cards. That was the first time since he was admitted to the hospital that I felt at peace. I knew he was there. I knew he was okay. The walls between some of my relatives and I melted away. The same love and joy I experienced with my Tatay was emitting from them.

After the nine-day prayer came the delegation of the different areas in preparation of the funeral. Aunty Fely took care of the fiscal and logistic arrangements. My cousin Eileen, took charge of the program. I sought to write and deliver Tatay's eulogy, and my cousin Alyssa would do the slideshow. So much thought had gone into how his body would be presented and what we need to do for him. Tatay was in a slicked-back, aloha shirt and trucker hat wearing barok. This would be one of the very few times we would adorn him in an ash gray suit. Tatay was a fisherman. All he would talk about during his last days were about all the monamon (tiny fish) he could see. We decided that his net and fishing pole would be fitting items to be buried with him.

I never thought that I would be playing the role that I did during the end of his life. I never thought that his sudden change in my life would occur simultaneously with the change I had initially been preparing for. The future seemed so bright and bleak at the same time. This bittersweet time in my life taught me to appreciate the time I have with my elders, to constantly ask for their knowledge and wisdom.

If I could see my Tatay right now, he'd probably be

squatting under the coconut tree outside his home just thinking. The home in which he'd have celebration for everything – from winning a chicken fight to a good catch. He was a family man, always wanting to make sure we would come together often to never lose touch. He was a gentle man, always looking to teach and never scold when we did wrong. He was a wise man, using his skills in farming and fishing to build his livelihood for him.

My Tatay was my torch in this world, accepting my "westernization," yet he was able to foster my pride and love of my Filipino heritage. This heritage has taught me the value of having a close family to spend every moment with. It has helped me to cherish the moments with my elders, for they have a wealth of knowledge to share. It has also led me to understand the importance of work ethic in that I should work hard in silence and let my success be the noise. I hope to be those same pillars to my children, grandchildren, and great grandchildren.

I miss you, Tatay. I'll see you where the monamon are.

Rebecca Carino was raised by first-generation immigrant parents from Laoag and Manila. Raised in a proudly Filipino family, she speaks Ilokano and Tagalog and continues to practice what her grandparents did before arriving in Hawai'i. She received her Bachelors of Arts in Humanities with a concentration in English from UH West Oahu, and is graduate student in Communications at UH Manoa.

Twenty Six
ANOTHER BEAUTIFUL DAY IN PARADISE: AUGUST 23, 2004
by Maiana Minahal

Even though I'd arrived in Hawai'i three days earlier, I still hadn't gone swimming with my father, which was one of our all-time favorite activities. My parents were enjoying their retirement and had been living in Hawai'i for the two months before my older brother Ray's wedding in Honolulu, now only a week away. My two younger brothers, Alan and Michael, their significant others, and assorted family members were flying into the Honolulu Airport throughout the week to attend the wedding. I was the first of the out-of-towners to arrive, so I could hang out with my parents during the day, then crash on their living room couch at night. I was anticipating the celebration with a mixture of excitement and nervousness.

My father declared himself as an expert at evading the crowds of tourists who swarmed the Waikiki beaches. He decided that we'd go for a swim after breakfast on Monday morning. My parents' air-conditioned one-bedroom apartment in the Discovery Bay condominiums was decorated in a typical 1970s beach style: Tropical flower wallpaper in pastel lavender and sage, matching floor-length curtains framing the glass sliding doors of the lanai, creamy pink linoleum in the bathroom. I sat up from the couch from under the covers I'd slept in the night before, and heard my parents speaking in Visayan to each other. Mom was boiling oatmeal in the kitchen, while Pop read the newspaper, spread out on the dining table. Over the paper, in his left hand, he passed a magnifying glass,

215

the same one he had used to read the *Los Angeles Times* with when we were teenagers growing up. I stretched and yawned. Pop looked over at me.

"You awake now?" he asked.

"Umnhh," I grunted.

"It's early yet, so the ocean water is cold, but it will get warm soon." He put the magnifying glass down, and turned towards me in his chair. "One thing I've found about Hawai'i, it's cold for a short time in the morning, but it does not stay cold."

"Just like the Philippines?" I asked.

"No." He smiled. "Better."

After we ate breakfast and changed into our swimming clothes, we took the elevator down three flights to the sidewalk, then walked one long block down Ala Moana Boulevard, which was always congested with tourist buses and traffic. On every other corner, there was an ABC store stocked with cheap enameled shell necklaces, fraying rainbow-colored fabric leis, and chocolate-covered macadamia nuts. We crossed the street at the first stoplight, then walked into the open-air shopping village that had been built around the towering Hilton Hotel complex. Bronze statues of mythic Hawaiian warriors and princesses greeted us at the entrance, frozen in frolic above the hotel sign. "They have fireworks here," Pop effused. "We only walk across the street, and we can watch them every night!" The mall shops were high-end jewelry stores and art galleries, catering to shoppers who were shaded from the Waikiki heat by covered walkways that connected to the hotel. Miniature tropical bird sanctuaries had been built into the corners. "Look, so beautiful!" Mom cooed, as we approached one. A crowd of hotel guests, hamming for photos to show to friends back home, had descended upon a group of tame, orange-pink flamingos that lived on the hotel property. The beautiful flamingos, with their s-shaped necks and beaks dipped in black, struck majestic poses against the rich green hues of the professionally landscaped scenery. But they jumped slightly, whenever anyone got too close, close enough to touch them.

We walked past the large hotel pools where guests sunned themselves in lounge chairs and reached the edge of the beach. A few sunburnt families stood in line at the towel stands. Tanned college boys in sunglasses manned the surfboard rentals, and a shirtless cyclist whizzed past on a bike. Scattered on the sand were vacationers from Idaho, tourists from Japan, newlyweds from Europe. Even though slight clouds were passing by overhead, the morning was promising to turn into another beautiful day in paradise. Mom put a wide-brimmed straw hat on her head, while Pop chose a spot for us next to a tall palm tree. I unfolded a towel on the white sand and relaxed. The ocean water was a blazing deep blue. Pop took out his camera.

"Take a picture of us," he told my mother. We sat close together on the towel.

"Cheese," Mom directed. She snapped a few photos. "I'm going back to the apartment while you swim. I will get too dark if I stay out here." Mom, vain Filipina that she was raised to be, always worried about keeping her skin as light as possible.

"Give her your phone and wallet," Pop said to me. He jumped up and shook the plastic slippers from his feet, while I remained sitting cross-legged on the towel. "So we don't have to worry. You know, so many people here just leave their things on the ground. You never know if your things will be here when you come back from swimming."

"But what if we need our stuff while we're out here?" I asked, looking up as I lazed on the towel.

"Never mind that," he said, "she'll come back before then." He scanned the ocean just past the shore, peering at the mild waves that swelled before crashing on the sand.

Mom put our cell phones and wallets in her purse, then threaded her way back through the throng of hotel guests and shops. Ignoring the book and writing journal in my bag, I laid

217

down on the towel under the sun. Pop took off his tee shirt and plunged into the ocean water. When he came out, I was reading my book. He plopped down next to me on the sand, his brown skin dripping with cool salt water.

"Boy, the water's nice," he panted. Flecks of water sparkled in his salt-and-pepper hair. He reached into his duffel bag, and pulled out a plastic snorkel hose and eye goggles.

"This really is the life, huh, Pop?" I asked.

"Yeah," he grinned, and took off to jump back in the water. His grin was ear to ear.

The sun was hot, the sand was hot.

Pop went back in the water, and I laid down on the towel. Through my closed eyelids, I could see the sunlight brighten and dim; clouds drifting in front of the sun. Suddenly, I started to feel uneasy. How long had Pop been swimming? I wanted to sit up and look out at the water. *Don't worry so much*, I thought to myself. *Pop's the strongest swimmer in the family. He's been swimming since he was a kid, even before I was born.* All the times we'd gone to the beach and he'd gone swimming in the ocean, in the Philippines as well as in the U.S., I'd never been worried before. So why should I start now?

I shook off the feeling and concentrated on enjoying the sun's warming rays. The smell of the sunscreen I'd applied earlier drifted in the breeze. I could hear people squealing, as waves splashed while they waded in the water's edge. For just a split second, there was a lull. The ocean's low roaring died down, and everything grew still.

"Call 911! Call 911!" a voice rang out sharply. I sat up. Further down the beach, two men on bright green and orange inflatable plastic floats were paddling towards the shore. Then I saw Pop. But why is one of the men towing his body alongside his plastic float? Why is that man holding him up above the surface of the water? They were closing in to the shore. I jumped up, sand flying from my heels as I ran. When I reached them, the two men were dragging my father's body onto the

218

beach. His limbs flopped limply onto the ground. "Pop!" I yelled, as I fell onto my knees, half-covering him with my shadow. His neck was slack, and his face was tilted to the side. I leaned over him. Although his eyes were open, there was no sign of recognition. Even from where I had been lying on my towel, I had been able to see that his stomach was enormously bloated, but now, kneeling next to him, I realized that it was swollen to a size I had never imagined possible. I felt sick.

A middle-aged woman with bleached blonde hair and a young man wearing shorts and a cut-off tee shirt stood above us on the sand. The blonde woman crouched down and squeezed Pop's wrist, checking for a pulse. She didn't look at me. My heart started racing. *Oh no, oh no,* I thought. *This can't be happening.* Without a word, she turned Pop over onto his stomach, while the young man watched. Pop's head flopped to the side, facing me. His eyes were open, but they didn't move. Could he see me? Could he see anything at all? The blonde pressed down on his back. His body heaved forward and—of his own accord, or because of the pressure she exerted, I couldn't tell—ocean water and shiny slivers of phlegm gushed out of his mouth. Panic rose in my chest. I took short, sharp breaths. The gritty sand scraped against my knees. I saw Pop's right hand lying quietly on the sand. It was still cold from the ocean when I picked it up. "Breathe, Pop," I said forcefully, looking into his eyes, searching for light. "Breathe."

"Turn him on his back," the woman told the young man. She still hadn't said a word to me. The young man turned Pop's body over. He got on his knees, and started pumping Pop's chest in a regular rhythm with his hands clasped, while the woman timed the chest presses with her watch.

"One. Two."

Pop's head was back, his mouth open. Ocean water pooled in the back of his throat.

"Six. Seven."

"Breathe, Pop," I repeated. My voice grew more

insistent. More panicked. "Breathe."

"Thirteen. Fourteen."

I looked into his eyes. *Please, give me a flicker of response, the slightest sign of anything. Any movement at all. Anything.*

"Nineteen. Twenty."

Above Pop's unblinking eyes, near his eyelashes, I noticed some grains of sand stuck to his forehead. *Was that from when they turned him over? Was it chafing his skin?*

"Twenty four."

I held his hand in mine, repeating the words over and over again. "Breathe, Pop. Breathe. Breathe. Breathe."

"Thirty." The young man pinched Pop's nose, then blew breaths into his mouth. He held his ear to Pop's mouth. He looked up at the woman.

She looked at her watch, and started counting again. "One. Two."

All three of us looked up when we heard clanging. Two sweating emergency medical technicians, dressed in white, struggled towards us in the soft sand, dragging a gurney between them. The metal-tipped straps of the gurney banged against its metal bars, as the IV bag above them swung back and forth. The hot sun flashed on their sunglasses. Seeing them, I had a vague memory of hearing distant sirens wailing, in between the woman's counting. Intent as I was on Pop, I hadn't looked up at all, and only now did I notice that everyone on the beach had turned towards us, fixed on the unfolding events. *It's like they're watching a car crash, and they can't help it,* I realized, horrified. *Except this car crash is Pop.*

The EMTs dropped the gurney and crouched down on the sand next to us. The woman and young man stood up. I wanted to breathe a sigh of relief. *EMTs are professionals,* I thought. *They'll know what to do. They'll fix this.* I looked into Pop's motionless eyes again. I was still holding his hand. I blundered through their questions.

"Does he have any medical conditions?"

"What was he doing?"

"Who found him?"

"How long was he out there?"

My brain was foggy. I couldn't remember, I didn't know how to answer. "No, I don't think he has any medical conditions." How could I not remember his medical conditions? "Oh, wait, he has high blood pressure." What was wrong with me? Both of my parents had started taking high blood pressure medicine when I was in high school; Pop swallowed a few white pills every day. How could I have forgotten? "Oh yeah, he has high blood pressure. But that's it. He's healthy otherwise." How could I have forgotten this? What kind of daughter was I?

The EMTs pulled out a pair of electrodes that were wired to a small defibrillator machine. I let go of Pop's hand and stood up. The older EMT gripped the grey plastic handles and placed the padded part of the electrodes against Pop's chest. The younger guy stood behind him, making room between us. "Clear," he called out. Suddenly, Pop's body shuddered on the sand as the electric current ran through him. Then his limbs lay slack. They tried again. "Clear!" Nothing. Dumbfounded, I looked at the EMTs. They started packing up the defibrillator. My father still lay motionless on the sand.

I dropped to my knees by Pop's side, and picked up his hand. It was still cold. His eyes were still open, unblinking. The EMTs were hovering, doing nothing. Leaning over my father's motionless body, I scanned his face. *How long had it been since he'd come out of the water?* I calculated quickly. *Three minutes of CPR...or four minutes? Then with the EMTs, four minutes? So eight minutes so far?* Panic was cresting quickly, about to take me under. *How many minutes does it take for brain damage? Four, or five? Even less?*

Then, in his jaw, something changed. The muscles slackened, ever so slightly, almost as if his entire face relaxed, for just a fraction of a millimeter or so. It was barely a loosening around his mouth, so small and minute, but just enough of an opening to release one, last, almost breath. Just enough to spirit him away. Suddenly my panic spiked. Suddenly the heat from the sun felt stifling, and my breathing grew sharp, shallow. I looked away from Pop's body, and up into the sky, directly at the sun. The light blinded me. I closed my eyes. Here was my father's body. At the center of some spinning circle that I was now part of, as if some hand in the universe had scooped us up, shook the ground beneath our feet, and tossed us here on this shore, almost as if shaking out a blanket. And now, we were tumbling. I held Pop's cold, motionless hand, and the panic in my chest burst into loud, jagged sobs. And everyone on the beach, the medical personnel in their official uniforms, the gawking tourists, together we were all spinning, faster and faster, around the axis of my father's lifeless, brown body.

 *Maiana Minahal is a teacher, interdisciplinary artist, and author of the chapbooks "Closer" and "Sitting Inside Wonder" (Monkey Press), and a full-length poetry collection, "Legend Sondayo." Born in Manila and raised in Los Angeles, she received her MFA from Antioch University. She currently teaches English and Writing at Kapi'olani Community College.*

Twenty Seven
DEAR MINDANAO
by Geraldine Ilan

Dear Mindanao,

Let me introduce myself,
Ang pangalan ko ay Geraldine Dadulla Ilan
Pero ang tawag sa akin ng pamilya ko ay Denden
Ang tatay ko ay taga Pangasinan
At ang nanay ko ay taga Ilocos Norte

Pasensiya na sa Tagalog ko
I apologize for the brokenness
Hidden behind my Filipino-American accent

I don't speak much Filipino,
But understanding a bit of the Tagalog dialect
It's the closest to the Filipino language I could possibly get
You can say that I'm still in the process of learning
And I'm still trying to reconnect with a culture
I've lost basis with
Even before the day I was born

I was brought into this world
By my parents
As a second-generation Filipina
And I am so grateful
Nagpapasalamat ako
Kasi nag tatrabaho ang aking pamilya
Para sa akin

223

My family had to go through so many hardships
Just for me to have the American dream
Already at my finger tips

But because they wanted the best for me
I have become blinded to the fact
That my veins
Are still tied to my ancestors
Who cared for the land that you call your home

Mindanao,
Pasensya na hindi ako nandiyan sa 'Pinas
I'm sorry for being too far away from the battle
And for not being able to help you fight
In this civil war
I never learned how to be a super hero
And you never deserved to become the damsel in distress
But I will still do my best to fight for you

Kung sinabi kong "Makikipaglaban ako para sa iyo"
Ang ibig kong sabihin
"Gagamit ko ang aking mga salita para sa 'yo"

So please wait for me
Hintayin mo ako

When I say that I will fight for you
I will fight using my words
As ammunition
And spread the news that there are problems like this
happening in our   country
I will make people aware that you are in need of help too

So please
Stay strong
And stand up for what is yours

 *Geraldine Dadulla Ilan, also known as Denden, is a Filipino-America poet who was born and raised on the island of Oahu. Her parents migrated from the Philippines. She moved from the streets of Kalihi to the small town of Waipahu at a young age. Currently, she is studying at Hawai'i Pacific University and is pursuing a bachelor's degree in Business, with the concentration of Hospitality and Tourism Management, while also striving for a minor in Japanese.*

Twenty Eight
LIFE IS A PRAYER
by reyna aiko leah lani ramolete hayashi

Manong Onel welcomed me into his home
We sat down at the wooden table
to share pagkain, kuwentuhan,
to bear witness,
Just as we were about to eat, Manong Onel said,
"I don't know your religion or if you pray before you eat.
I do not pray before I eat.
My life is a prayer."

My life is a prayer.
One simple truth.
Uttered in passing, without agenda or ego, as Manong Onel
scooped rice onto his plate.

What if life was a prayer?
What if we raised our foreheads to father sky
letting his raindrops baptize our spirit?

What if life was a prayer?
What if fields of kamote, mais, palay, kalabasa
brought us to our knees at the soil's altar each morning?
What if each bead of sweat rolling off our weathered brown
bodies
was the holy water anointing each seed we planted?

What if life was a prayer?
What if the smoke from our fire,
repelling bugs while we tended the fields,
dancing with the dawn's arms reaching through the forest
canopy,
was the holy incense that sanctified our lungs?

What if life was a prayer?
What if every meal we ate was communion,
not a noun but a verb,
each grain of palay, a sacred communing,
our physical body becoming one
with the collective body of our family, our tribe, our mother
earth?

What if life was a prayer?
What if our confession was a shared space,
our act of asking for forgiveness a community matter?
What if to restore balance for our wrongs
our tribe sent us to work the communal farm as our penance?
And our repentance was to weed out the invasives, to unearth
and nourish all that is native in us, native to our bodies, native
to our ecosystems?

What if life was a prayer?
What if the hundreds of rings in the trunks of trees
were our Bible and our history book,
and we kept them alive to listen to their hushed sermon?
What if we could read the i-jiu's flight patterns and the stars
as scripture?
Would we have the faith to navigate the Pacific to a group of
mother islands we hadn't seen but felt?

What if life was a prayer?
What if instead of a nameless holy spirit
the familiar faces and voices of our ancestors

were our anito, our spirit guides?
What if we could read their omens
in the intestines of animal sacrifice?
What if the omens told us
of the boots of soldiers,
of the smoke of villages burning,
of the bullet holes in classrooms,
of children screaming,
of the rivers running red,
of the blood of teachers and elders soaking our ancestral land?
What then?
Would we pray
or would we live?

What if life was a prayer?
What if the earth was our temple,
our grocery store,
our freshwater spring,
our bathtub,
our laundry mat,
our hospital,
our playground,
our library,
our teacher,
our memory,
our Lola?

What if she was under attack
brutally raped by foreign loggers, miners, and money?
What if the military turned our temple into a war zone,
torturing and murdering our leaders, our teachers, our loved
ones?
What if you and 4,000 of our people were violently forced off
our ancestral lands
into a sports complex turned evacuation camp in the city?
What if we were no longer called by our names,

but instead internally displaced peoples, refugees, bakwit?
Would we pray to a god separate from ourselves?
Would we make demands of those in power,
the very people that robbed us of our culture for tourism,
called us communist rebels to justify their civil war,
trained soldiers to murder our leaders for land grabbing?
Would we petition those same people to stop the ethnocide, the ecocide they created?

Or

Would we defend the trees as our sisters and brothers?
Would we carry our slain leaders on our backs for miles into the city in soundless protest?
Would our teachers hold art therapy at the refugee camp?
Would our students heal each others' bodies with hilot?
Would our children sing tudom and freedom songs?
Would our youth perform balagtasan and street theatre to educate the masses about our movement?
Would our artisans harvest rattan and weave dudong to sell?
Would our farmers plant seeds in the dirt at the refugee camp?

Would we see far enough
into ten thousand tomorrows,
into one hundred generations,
to live our life as a prayer,
to learn how to become not a good person, but a good ancestor,
to look deeply into the eyes of our great great great grandchildren,
to build alternative indigenous schools,
to arm our children with
our kultura,
our resistance,
our freedom.

What if life was a prayer?
And we were being made, moment by moment, by the movement
And no matter how far to the edges of mother earth we were pushed,
we could know sovereignty,
because it was a practice, not a prayer,
And we already, always, and after
embodied the same freedom we were fighting for?

What if life was a prayer
And our ancestors prayed, chanted, willed us into existence
And we were the answer to their prayers?

This poem is dedicated to our beloved kasama "Emuk" Emerito Samarca, Executive Director of ALCADEV (Alternative Learning Center for Agricultural and Livelihood Development); "Onel" Dionel Campos, Chairman of MAPASU, an organization that fights for land and human rights; and Datu "Bello" Juvello Sinzo. All devoted their lives to the struggle of the Lumad, the indigenous people of Mindanao. They were assassinated by paramilitary troops in the province of Surigao del Sur in 2015.

The poem is also for the students, teachers, farmers, and families of sitio Han-ayan, ALCADEV, and TRIFPSS (Tribal Filipino Program of Surigao del Sur) who are fighting for their right to education, self-determination, and defending their yutang kabilin (ancestral lands) from mining and militarization.

Reyna Aiko Leah Lani Ramolete Hayashi was born and raised in Kapālama on Oahu, Hawai'i. Her ancestors are from Ilocos Sur, Philippines and Japan. She is a graduate of Moanalua High School, University of British Columbia, and Seattle University School of Law where she was a Scholar for Justice. She works as a community lawyer at the Legal Aid Society of Hawai'i doing community education, advocacy, and civil rights litigation. Reyna's work and life is guided by her anito, her Nanay, weekends with her Lola and Lolo in Waipahu, her loving, powerful, and resilient community of 'ohana and friends, and her deep reverence for the ea of the place that raised her, Hawai'i.

Twenty Nine
HOME

by Marie Antonette Anamong Ramos

My home
lies within the 7,000+
islands of the Philippines.

Luzon. Mankayan, Benguet.

Although raised on
the beautiful island of Oahu,
I've never once forgotten
where I come from

My mother's land *is* my
mother land and
because of her
I can say that we are
mountain people

Igorots

Stereotyped by our dark
skin, rough hands
and calloused feet
we have been made
laughing stocks
by other Filipinos

But regardless of the labels
that have been placed upon us
(*uneducated, lazy, backward, savages*)

We have held
our heads up high
and our backs erected.

The same backs that have been
disciplined to withstand
endless hours of tending
fields and harvesting crops.

The same backs that have carried
　generations after
　　generations after
　　　after generations of future –

　　　　warriors,
　　　　weavers,
　　　　dancers,
　　　　storytellers,
　　　　spiritual doctors,
　　　　and great leaders

We have thrived for centuries
high up in our mountains
　　built by our hands
lies the 8th wonder of the world –
　　a stairway of rice terraces
　　for ascension of spirits.

They will claim our
rice terraces as their own
but they refuse to claim its people

Marie Antonette Anamong Ramos was born in Baguio, Philippines to Sylvia and Antonio Ramos. She immigrated to Hawai'i with her family at the age of five, the beginning of her lifelong journey of navigating multiple identities and understanding the privileges/responsibilities of being: Filipino, Local, Igorot, Indigenous, American, and Pin@y. Her dream is to one day return "home."

Thirty
ANG DALAGANG PILIPINA
by Anna Davide

We have island gem archipelago glittering across our bones. Ageless. Forever strong. Skin golden from flying so high we have grazed the sun. Our scales are woven in with piña fiber into translucent cloth. Dressed in butterfly winged terno, Maria Clara, kimona. The rest of the world has not yet caught up with the genius of our canvas.

Golden filigree, tambourine medallions, and siopao pearls clad our necks and earlobes with unequaled elegance. We are women caressed in gold. Hair twisted up into a bun, we intertwine sweat from a day's labor with equal measure perfume. Yung amoy ng sampaguita (the smell of the sampaguita flower) that lingers after every embrace.

We possess a flame not to be forgotten. Our stories woven into our recipes, fashion, bodies. Sa aming halik (in our kiss) graced upon loved ones. A legacy embodied in our lives just by living.

I love my heritage so much I've cried. Proud to come from a bloodline mother of pearl luminescent from the Orient. A tenacity brazen throughout a nation.

Our myths, legends, heroines.

Maria Makiling: Diwata ng Laguna, whose body forms mountain tops overlooking the barangays. Gilded generosity, but be warned not to invite her scorn. Her many spirits roaming throughout the peaks turning ginger into gold, her whims control the weather, and is a force of nature all on her own.

Gabriela Silang: The revolutionary, rebel la generala, bolo-wielding widow on horseback. Bane of the Spanish authorities, leading the Ilokano independence movement for an immortal four months before her capture and execution.

Marcela Agoncillo: Once exiled from the homeland yet blessed to birth the first Philippine flag. The embodiment of our aspirations, embroidered in gold: Tatlong bituin at isang araw (three stars and one sun) cushioned in royal blue and scarlet.

Nieves Fernandez: School teacher and WWII guerrilla war leader during the Japanese occupation. She set DIY hellfire on the enemy, killing 200 Japanese soldiers with crude weaponry—knives and gas pipe shotguns. She was wounded only once by a bullet that grazed her right forearm.

President Corazon Aquino: The first female Asian president, leading the nation after the Marcos regime which assassinated her husband. She isn't recognized for a collection of 1,000 shoes, but rather the honor of being *Time* magazine's 1986 "Woman of the Year."

And my own Lola, Paula Athena, who hid her political activist niece whose husband, Satur Ocampo, was political prisoner, providing sanctuary for a mother and her children to meet.

We are not the Dalagang Filipina of *Noli Me Tangere*. We have never been demure, but dauntless. Never self-effacing, but self-sacrificing. Never anything less than heroine. We are freedom fighters. We are the revolutionary daughters, sisters, wives, and widows from a lineage of women warriors.

I have inherited the dragon blood of my ancestors. Our blood boiling, shedding own and those of others. Our souls sent as libations up to our Lupang Hinirang, our lives burning, our hearts beating, our tongues aflame, our wingbeats echoing a call for justice.

This is what it means to be Filipina. Ako ay Dalagang Filipina.

Anna Davide is a proud Filipina of Tagalog, Cebuano, and Lithuanian decent. In 2016, she graduated from Mililani High School as one of 56 valedictorians and with the honor of summa cum laude. Currently, she is perusing her undergraduate studies at the University of Hawai'i at Manoa. Beyond her academic pursuits, she explores her heritage through spoken word poetry and song.

ABOUT
THE FILIPINO ASSOCIATION OF UNIVERSITY WOMEN

Filipino Association
of University Women

The Filipino Association of University Women (FAUW) was established in 1987 to promote and strengthen Filipino identity in Hawai'i through initiatives in culture, the arts, and education. Since its inception, the organization has provided leadership in promoting greater awareness of and appreciation for the Filipino culture and values, and cross-cultural understanding in Hawai'i.

FAUW's programs include *Pasko!* a Christmas celebration; *Anak,* a children's festival; and the sponsorship of film festivals, art tours and exhibits, literacy projects, and cultural displays. FAUW has partnered with organizations such as the Honolulu Museum of Arts, the Children's Discovery Center, the Filipino Community Center, the University of Hawai'i Center for Philippine Studies, the Philippine Consulate General of Hawai'i; the Friends of the Iolani Palace, and Reiyukai Hawai'i.

Its primary publications are *From Mabuhay to Aloha*, Jovy Zimmermann, editor (1989); *Voices of the Youth* (anthology of literary works of students of Filipino ancestry, (1990); *Filipina,* Pepi Nieva, editor (1992); *Kayumangi Presence*, Pepi Nieva, editor (1992); *Lola Basyang, Volumes 1 and 2* (DVD – various storytellers; Ruth Mabanglo, project director, 2010 and 2011). *PINAY: Culture Bearers of the Filipino Diaspora* is the organization's fifth print publication. In 2016, the group also helped launch two books on World War II that was written or edited by its members.

FAUW is a tax-exempt organization. Tax-deductible donations support FAUW projects and can be sent via PayPal (email: fauw1987@gmail.com).

For membership and more information, visit us on Facebook (FAUW) and our website: fauwhawaii.wordpress.com

ABOUT THE BOOK COVER DESIGNER

Maria Katrina "Kit" Zulueta was born in Baguio City and grew up in Bataan and Quezon City, Philippines. She graduated cum laude with a degree in Film from the University of the Philippines Diliman, then moved to Hawai'i in 2008. She has taken various leadership roles with the County of Maui government and with local and national community groups such as the Maui Filipino Chamber of Commerce and the Filipino Young Leaders Program of the Philippine Department of Foreign Affairs.

She owns a creative company called Kit Zulueta Products LLC, teaches karate, enjoys travel and farming, and loves cats. You can find her @keeet.

CPSIA information can be obtained
at www.ICGtesting.com
Printed in the USA
LVHW082322120622
721101LV00031B/943

9 781542 329873